DISCARD

THE
FACE OF
MONARCHY

THE
FACE
OF

Richard Ormond

MONARCHY

British royalty portrayed

PHAIDON *Oxford* · E. P. DUTTON *New York*

PHAIDON PRESS LIMITED
Littlegate House, St Ebbe's Street, Oxford

Published in the United States of America by
E. P. DUTTON, NEW YORK

First published 1977
© 1977 by Phaidon Press Limited
All rights reserved

ISBN 0 7148 1762 7

Library of Congress Catalog Card
Number : 77-71182

Filmset and printed in Great Britain by
BAS Printers Limited, Wallop,
Hampshire

Contents

For Leonée

Preface

I MUST FIRST RECORD MY DEBT to those pioneers in the study of royal iconography on whom my book leans heavily, especially Sir Oliver Millar and Dr Roy Strong, whose publications figure frequently in my notes. I must also acknowledge the unfailing help and support of Keith Roberts, who initiated the project with me and helped to select the plates. I am indebted for picture research and editorial assistance to Anne Dean, Sabine MacCormack and Jane Rendel of Phaidon Press. Great service has been rendered by those who have supplied photographs, especially the staff of the Lord Chamberlain's Office, and that of the National Portrait Gallery publications department. Her Majesty the Queen has graciously consented to the reproduction of a great many portraits in the Royal Collection. I should like to express my gratitude to her and to the many other owners acknowledged in the notes to the plates. Finally I must thank those who supported me at home and made the project possible.

Richard Ormond
HIGHGATE, 1976

Introduction

OUR KINGS AND QUEENS have been a source of awe and fascination from early times. Figures of remote magnificence and the focus of elaborate ceremonials, they are the supreme embodiment of the state, raised far above their fellow creatures. So powerful is the mystique surrounding them that even today a royal personage or event attracts excited interest. We continue to be moved by the monarchy and its atmosphere of pageantry long after it has lost all semblance of real power and authority.

Our conception of monarchy owes much to the tradition of royal portraiture. We see reflected there the outward pomp and circumstance of the king's estate. A royal portrait is instantly recognizable for what it is, and we are more familiar with its symbols than with the faces of most British monarchs. The present book is concerned primarily with the tradition of royal image-making, the development of the state portrait, and the role of the court painter. But it also attempts to bring the individual monarch to life, by looking beyond the stereotyped formal portrait to more personal characterizations. The book strikes a balance between the need, on one hand, to stress the continuity of royal portrait patterns, and, on the other, to give full weight to individual taste and idiosyncrasy. The field of royal portraiture is a vast one, and the present survey can claim to be no more than a summary and highly selective introduction to it.

Medieval kings & queens

Most people have an image of the early medieval kings that derives, not from any contemporary source, but from those historical pictures and prints whose appeal has lasted from the nineteenth century to this. There we see the kings in scenes sacred to popular tradition: William the Conqueror clasping the crown at his coronation; William Rufus meeting his end in the New Forest, shot down by an arrow; Henry II flagellating himself for the murder of Thomas à Becket; and Richard Cœur de Lion in captivity recognizing the song of his friend, Blondel. In the same way our view of the later medieval kings is inevitably coloured by Shakespeare's history plays, where they are strongly projected as individuals. In stepping behind these later images, we shall encounter the much less human and, indeed, rather bleak facts of the middle ages.

The few surviving representations of early medieval kings and queens provide evidence of the visual symbolism traditionally associated with the monarchy, but they have almost no significance as portraits. The idea of recording the likeness of a particular individual was alien to the medieval mind, which viewed man as the lowest form of creation in a universe dominated by the idea of God. The sculpture of the early medieval period can sometimes surprise us with the uncanny realism of certain figures and heads, but recognition of a particular person was never intended. The sculptor made use of familiar models to convey his message as vividly as possible.

Representations of early English kings figure on objects associated with the royal administration, like coins, seals, and charters, but as token symbols only. There is no attempt to give the human form any individuality. What was important was the office of kingship and its continuity. The regalia have now become ornamental trappings, but they had an almost totem-like significance in medieval times. They imparted to the person who wore them a sacred status. The new king could not be acknowledged until presented to his people in the coronation mantle, with the crown, orb, sceptre and sword of state. Hence the almost universal habit of representing the king with the regalia, to emphasize the powers vested in him by Church and state. The potent image of the king enthroned in majesty has persisted in royal portraiture from the very beginning down to the present day, and it is still one which can arouse an immediate response (*Plates 20, 26, 94 and 123*).

The most widespread use of the king's image in early medieval times occurs on coins. An efficient and centrally controlled coinage is an essential ingredient of economic and financial stability, and the presence of the king's head is a token of authenticity, and a reminder of royal prerogative. The history of the coinage, like that of other economic institutions, has been an erratic one. Monetary reforms were followed by periods of gradual debasement, affecting the content of silver and the quality of craftsmanship. Coins were minted in various parts of the country, usually from dies provided by the royal goldsmith. Changes in type occur from time to time, for reasons which are not clear, although they may be associated with periodic mint assays to test the quality of the coin.

Without the help of inscribed names, it would be difficult to tell one king from another on the coinage. Features are no more than a series of blobs for eyes, nose and mouth, and the design follows a limited range of patterns. The king, wearing a crown and holding a sceptre, is shown on the obverse, either full face or in profile, with his name inscribed round the rim. The reverse usually bears a decorated cross with a second inscription. It is significant that the coinage of William the Conqueror (*Plate 5*) differs little from that of his Saxon predecessors, and that no attempt is made to distinguish his coinage from that of his son, William II (*Plate 6*), by the addition of a numeral. The number and variety of types in the coinage of Henry I (*Plate 8*) is exceptionally large, perhaps an indication of economic prosperity and good housekeeping. The coinage of Stephen (*Plate 9*), minted during conditions of civil strife, shows a marked decline in standards of design and workmanship. Henry II (*Plate 10*) introduced the type called 'Tealby', from the large hoard found there in 1807, soon after his accession in 1154, and the short-cross issue, which replaced it in 1180, lasted well into the thirteenth century. The coins minted during the reigns of Richard I and John continue to bear the name of their father, Henry II.

Seals are a more elaborate expression of the powers vested in the monarchy, but they are no more illuminating as portraits. The practice of stamping documents with a wax impression from a seal to validate it is very ancient. A change of seal invariably accompanies a change of ruler. Only in this way can the new king demonstrate his succession and his legal right to command. As an instrument of government, the seal has always been of the greatest importance, and its care and protection are vested in the highest officers of state. The practice of attaching the seal to the document by means of a thong led to the use of the counter-seal as a reverse image. The seal of William the Conqueror (*Plate 4*) shows him mounted on horseback as a military leader on one side and enthroned on the other. Though stylistically more advanced than the Germanic-style seal employed by Edward the Confessor, its imagery is similar. No doubt William was anxious to stress political continuity, but seals are in general conservative and archaic in design. The use of a traditional pattern reinforces the monarchical and dynastic idea. The seals of William's successors are closely related to his in style and imagery (*Plate 7*), while developing more elaborate forms. The decisive change in seal design occurs in the reign of Henry II, when a striving for classical elegance replaces the essentially linear style of the Norman period (see F. Saxl, *English Sculptures of the Twelfth Century*, 1954).

Kings and queens have been represented on seals and coins from time immemorial to the twentieth century. Manuscript illumination, on the other hand, is an art particularly associated with the middle ages. The majority of texts were theological, and it follows that the monks who illuminated them were limited, by and large, to religious subjects and motifs. Scenes in which contemporary kings appear usually have an ecclesiastical context. They may be shown granting a charter to the monastery from which the manuscript originated, or they may appear in the role of donors if the manuscript was commissioned by them. But apart from inscriptions, and the context of the manuscript, they are no more identifiable than biblical kings and saints, whom they closely resemble. They are simply schematic figures wearing a crown and carrying the regalia. It is not until the fifteenth century that a humanistic concern with the appearance of the individual transforms kings from stereotypes into recognizable human beings (*Plates 28 and 30*).

Before leaving the subject of pictorial images, some mention must be made of the Bayeux Tapestry. This unique and extraordinary survival tells the story of the Norman Conquest in a thin narrative strip two hundred and thirty feet long (*Plate 3*). It was woven within living memory of the events it depicts, and it is full of energy and action. Each incident leading up to the Battle of Hastings is recorded in great detail, with an accompanying caption. Though we shall look in vain for a portrait of the Conqueror, the Bayeux Tapestry must rank as the first pictorial biography of an English king. The designer drew extensively on his knowledge of contemporary life, and the tapestry is remarkable for its largely secular imagery. The absence of familiar religious motifs has led some recent critics to question the assumption that it was commissioned by William's brother, Bishop Odo, for his new cathedral at Bayeux. They suggest that it was probably intended as a decoration for a large domestic building, perhaps the bishop's palace.

If we see the living king only in the most symbolic and stylized of images, what of the dead king? At the Abbey of Fontevrault, in what was then Anjou, lie the earliest surviving effigies of English kings, and they make a profoundly moving impression in the austere setting of this great Romanesque abbey (*Plate 11*). Represented are the first of the Plantaganets, Henry II (*Plate 12*), with his queen, Eleanor of Aquitaine, their eldest son, Richard Cœur de Lion, and their daughter-in-law, Isabella of Angoulême, the wife of King John (*Plates 13 and 14*). Their importance in the history of tomb sculpture is considerable, because for the first time the figures are treated as though they were dead, rather than as living figures placed unconvincingly in a recumbent pose. There is little doubt that these effigies represent the kings and queens as they were carried to burial, a point emphasized by the draped *lits de parade* on which they lie. The modelling of the features is flat and lightly incised (*Plate 12*), and it is doubtful if the sculptor was aiming at anything more than a conventional representation of a dead person. We are still a long way from the idea of the portrait.

The tombs of the later Plantaganets are among the most important surviving works of medieval sculpture. With the exception of Edward I, whose tomb is destroyed, all the kings and many of their queens are represented by effigies. One of the finest is that of King John at Worcester, a masterpiece of the Purbeck school (*Plate 15*). The head is powerfully modelled, but, as it is posthumous, one should not read too much into it as a likeness. Lawrence Stone, the historian of medieval art, points out that the squat head with its close-cropped beard is a standard feature of later Purbeck effigies.

The tombs of Henry III, John's son and successor, and of Henry's daughter-in-law, Eleanor of Castile, are the first for which there is any contemporary documentation. They were commissioned by Edward I, Henry III's son, in 1291, as part of a programme of dynastic glorification. The artist was a London goldsmith, William Torel, and the effigies (*Plates 16, 17 and 18*) represent something of a technical triumph: they are apparently the first full-length figures to be cast in bronze in England, and the quality of craftsmanship is very high. The flowing lines of the sculpture are sharp and elegant, and the chased decoration on the cushions of both effigies and the feet of Henry is superb. Stylistically they are rather old-fashioned, but in terms of technical virtuosity there is nothing comparable, and Lawrence Stone has written of the Eleanor, the finer of the two, that 'it represents the highest achievement of the idealistic preoccupations of the mid thirteenth century, modified by a hint of movement both of form and of line'.

Similarly idealistic is the effigy of Edward II, Edward I's tragic and inept son and successor, who was murdered by his wife, Isabella, and by her lover, Edmund Mortimer. The intense, almost anguished expression of the features seem strangely appropriate to what we know of Edward's life and character, but the effigy (*Plate 22*) was posthumous, and the face conforms to conventional representations of Christ. Edward enjoyed the status of a martyr, and his tomb (*Plate 19*) was the focus of a cult, which explains the explicitly religious nature of the image.

With the tomb effigy of Edward III one enters the sphere of portraiture for the first time (*Plate 23*). There seems little doubt that the head derives from that of the wooden funeral effigy at Westminster Abbey (*Plate 24*), almost certainly the one commissioned from Stephen Hadley and carried at Edward's funeral; the practice of showing an image of the dead king rather than his actual corpse may be traced back to the funeral of Henry III. It has been plausibly suggested that the head of the wooden effigy is based on a death mask, since the twisted expression of the mouth apparently records the effect of a stroke Edward is known to have suffered before he died. When the sculptor came to make the tomb effigy, he had to hand an obvious model from which to work. Although the likeness was still made subservient to the demands of style and technique, one can recognize the gaunt, long drawn out features of the wooden head.

In the case of Richard II, Edward's grandson and heir, we should have to rely on the evidence of sculpture once again, were it not for the existence of two absolutely unique painted images. It is a measure of their rarity that almost no other identifiable painted portraits of English kings are known to exist before the late fifteenth century. The earliest is the full-length in Westminster Abbey (*Plates 25 and 26*), a stiff and hieratic work, that conforms very much to the treatment of figures in contemporary religious painting. Yet, in spite of damage and overpainting, the head retains a sense of individual character, with its delicate, pointed features, and there seems little doubt that it was painted in Richard's lifetime as a recognizable likeness.

The so-called '*Wilton Diptych*' (*Plate 27*) is later, possibly posthumous. Richard II is presented to the Virgin and Child by his patron saints, while on the reverse of the diptych is a white hart (Richard's badge), and a shield with the arms of Edward the Confessor impaling those of the kingdom. No entirely convincing explanation of the picture's purpose and origin has yet been put forward, and many of its visual allusions remain obscure. Although seen in profile, the face of the king agrees well with the earlier full-length painting, and with the tomb effigy, both in Westminster Abbey. As a work of art the '*Wilton Diptych*' is of outstanding quality, and nothing comparable in England survives from the same period.

There is one further image of Richard that deserves consideration. This is the stained glass window in Winchester College Chapel, showing him kneeling before John the Baptist (originally part of the east window, now in the west window of Thurben's chantry). The glass was executed around 1393, within Richard's lifetime, and comparison with other portraits of him suggests that this was more than a merely conventionalized rendering. Kings, of course, appear quite frequently in stained glass, but usually as part of a hieratic series. The set of sixteen English kings commissioned for the Library of All Souls, Oxford by Henry VI is a good example. Included are Henry's immediate forbears, and those more ancient Anglo-Saxon kings, whose saintly lives might be considered a credit to the monarchical principle. The figures are, however, indistinguishable, and without the aid of inscriptions (in some cases obscured), it would be impossible to identify them. The naturalism found in the image of Richard II does not recur until the end of the fifteenth century, in the stained glass window at Canterbury depicting Edward IV and his family (*Plate 33*), and in various representations of Henry VII, Elizabeth of York, and their eldest son, Prince Arthur (Christ's College Chapel, Cambridge; St Giles's Church, Little Malvern, and elsewhere).

After the number and variety of Richard II's portraits, those of his successors come as a sad anticlimax. Henry IV is known only through the tomb of himself and his queen at Canterbury (*Plate 29*). With its intricate detail, this double tomb is a splendid example of the virtuosity achieved by the alabaster carvers in the late Gothic period. But the force and simplicity of Edward II's tomb at Gloucester (*Plate 22*) is missing. The modelling is more realistic, the forms more fully realized, but the effect is heavy and nerveless— a style in decline.

Henry IV is not a king who has left much mark on history. His son, Henry V, on the other hand, is one of the most famous and popular of all English monarchs. The 'Henry V look', if one may call it that, is familiar to everyone (especially as embodied by Laurence Olivier in his film of the Shakespeare play), and yet the contemporary sources for it are very few. One of the best is the manuscript illumination reproduced here, which shows the king receiving Occleve's 'De Regimine Principum' from its author (*Plate 28*). Here is the clean-shaven, slightly ascetic face of the soldier-king, with his distinctive hairstyle, dressed in a long, fashionable red gown. The manuscript includes the famous portrait of Chaucer, whose appearance, Occleve tells us, he preserves for the benefit of posterity.

Henry V's characteristic pudding-bowl hairstyle is recorded in an oil painting, one of a set of early English kings and queens produced in the workshops of Tudor artists. Such sets, repetitive in type and mechanical in quality, continued to be manufactured well into the seventeenth century. The first king to be represented in these sets was usually Edward III, and in his case the image was based on the head of the tomb effigy (*Plate 23*). With subsequent monarchs, it is difficult to know what sources were used for their portraits. That of Henry IV, which only occurs in late sixteenth-century sets, is known to be false; it was lifted from a print of Charles VI of France with the addition of a beard. The profile pose of Henry V's portrait suggests that it may have been derived from a contemporary votive painting.

The earliest and best-preserved set of kings and queens is in the Royal Collection. While most of the portraits are of routine quality, like that of Henry VI, Henry V's son (*Plate 31*), the portrait of Edward IV (*Plate 32*), the Yorkist king who usurped his throne, is altogether more sensitive and refined. The discovery of a related engraving of about 1472 adds weight to the theory that the portrait is from life, possibly by a Flemish artist. It conveys something of the charm and sense of physical well-being which so impressed his contemporaries. According to Polydore Virgil, the Anglo-Italian historian, he was 'unusually handsome and pleasant of face, broad chested, well formed and so tall that his head and shoulders towered above those of nearly all other men'. Edward appears in a number of contemporary manuscripts, including Jean de Waurin's 'English chronicles', which he commissioned in Flanders during his brief exile there from 1470 to 1471 (*Plate 30*). The author is shown presenting his book to the king, who is attended by courtiers, one of them probably his brother, the notorious Richard of Gloucester, later Richard III. Edward and Richard were men of considerable culture, who patronized art and learning to a much greater degree than is generally realized. It is unfortunate that their portraiture is so limited. The standard portrait of Richard (*Plate 34*), again from a set of kings and queens, is undistinguished in quality. Richard's champions have often quoted the portrait as evidence of a benevolent disposition, but it is dangerous at the best of times to interpret character from portraiture, and especially here where the image is so wooden.

The Tudors

Richard was defeated and killed at the Battle of Bosworth in 1485 by the Lancastrian claimant, Henry Tudor, who succeeded as Henry VII. His reign marks the advent of a new age in art no less than in politics. The settled political climate, the growth of prosperity and renewed links with the

Continent, all played their part in drawing England back towards the mainstream of European art. Henry VII, and his son, Henry VIII, realized the importance of harnessing the arts to a programme of dynastic glorification. In this they were truly Renaissance in outlook, and it is not surprising to find artists of the calibre of Pietro Torrigiano, a Florentine, and Hans Holbein in service at their courts. Portraiture flourished as never before, and it is in the early sixteenth century that the state portrait first develops. The panel portrait in oils is almost unknown before 1500. By the end of the century the habit of being painted had become almost universal among the upper classes. In the long galleries of Tudor houses, the portrait collection takes shape, exemplifying pride of person, position and family.

It is significant that Henry VII, the founder of a new dynasty, should be commemorated in a tomb that sets a totally new precedent in English sculpture (*Plate 37*). Commissioned, in October 1512, from Torrigiano, the tomb, which shows Henry with his queen, Elizabeth of York, ranks as the first major Renaissance monument to be erected in this country. The marble tomb chest is decorated with Italianate figures and reliefs, while the effigies themselves are executed in bronze. The quality of workmanship is superb, and the naturalism of the heads and figures marks a break with the formalized conventions of medieval tomb sculpture. Henry is shown without any outward display of rank, in an attitude of private devotion, but there is no mistaking the air of majesty with which the sculptor has invested his figure. The use of ordinary costume is perhaps intended to show that Henry was a scholar and humanist as well as a great prince.

Torrigiano was probably the sculptor of the painted terracotta bust of Henry (*Plate 36*), which shows a similar treatment of features. The effect of the bust, however, is much more lifelike than the bronze effigy, and it conforms closely to the type of portrait bust which originated in Florence in the mid fifteenth century, at once monumental and realistic.

There is one outstanding painted image of Henry VII: the panel portrait by Michael Sittow (*Plate 35*). This was executed in 1505 during the marriage negotiations between Henry and the Emperor Maximilian, and it was given to Henry's intended bride, the emperor's daughter, Margaret of Savoy. Torrigiano's sculptures of Henry present us with a noble if somewhat severe Renaissance prince, and they appear positively idealized by the side of Sittow's subtle and idiosyncratic characterization. His portrait hints at some of the complexities of Henry's personality. An ironic air can be traced in the expressive line of the lips, reminding us of his detached and calculating nature. The hands rest delicately on the ledge in front of him, as if emerging illusionistically from the picture space. Such refinement is a feature of Flemish art, and by comparison with Sittow's sensitive portrait, those of Henry by English workshops look crude and lifeless.

The most interesting portraits of Henry VII were executed by foreigners, and they exerted no real influence on the development of royal portraiture in England. That honour belongs to Hans Holbein, the court painter of Henry VIII, and one of the outstanding masters of the northern Renaissance. Holbein's presence at court was not entirely a matter of chance, for Henry was one of the most discerning patrons of art ever to sit on the English throne. Foreign artists and craftsmen flocked to his court to help build and decorate the great series of palaces for which he is famous, Whitehall, Hampton Court and Nonsuch. In the course of a few years, England was exposed to the influence of first, Renaissance, and then mannerist art, at a speed which must have induced some degree of cultural shock. From its position as a Gothic backwater, England was suddenly in the van of the latest European styles.

Holbein first came to England in 1526, with a letter of introduction from Erasmus to Thomas More, whose portrait he painted, together with a family group. By the time that Holbein became Henry's official painter some ten years later, More was dead, and with him the hopes of English humanism. Holbein owed his introduction to court to Thomas Cromwell, Henry's ruthless servant who effected the breach with Rome and the dissolution of the monasteries. The great wall painting, which Holbein executed for the privy chamber in Whitehall Palace around 1536-7, can be linked with Cromwell's propaganda campaign to emphasize Henry's supremacy in Church and state. To convey the king's imperial pretensions, Holbein formulated an image entirely new to English royal portraiture. The fresco, now destroyed but known from a copy (*Plate 41*), depicted the full-length figures of Henry VIII and his father, Henry VII, on one side, and their two queens, Jane Seymour and Elizabeth of York, on the other. Henry VIII, in the forefront of the design, and the only figure looking directly out, dominated the group. His heroic and monumental pose was combined with an overpowering sense of physical reality. People entering the privy chamber were no doubt cowed by the image of this colossus, bearing down on them from above. So powerful was Holbein's pictorial imagination that he was able to create a definitive archetype. Though we know the fresco only at second hand, this is how we always visualize Henry, with his square bullet head, legs masterfully astride, dressed in a magnificent, jewelled costume.

Holbein's fresco is recorded in the original cartoon of the left-hand side, showing Henry VII and Henry VIII (*Plate 42*). Though rubbed and damaged, the cartoon is still astonishingly evocative, with its large forms and intricate linear patterns. There is a related half-length portrait of Henry VIII in the Thyssen-Bornemisza Collection (*Plate 39*), the only certain painting of him from Holbein's hand now surviving, and this has a similar solidity and force. There is nothing in the least intimate or revealing in Holbein's characterization, either here or in the cartoon, but he demonstrates the force of Henry's personality.

The English state portrait may be said to begin with Holbein's wall painting. There are several full-length portraits of the king copied from his figure in the fresco, which suggests that there existed an early demand for images of Henry, and perhaps a conscious policy of disseminating them (*Plate 40*). The Tudors were not slow to exploit the propaganda potential of portraiture. Holbein began the now ruined group of Henry and the Barber Surgeons, which is still owned by the Barbers Company, and possibly the portrait of him holding a staff, but in neither case did the king give him a special sitting, since the face patterns of both derive from the Whitehall fresco.

Apart from Henry, Holbein painted many of the leading figures of his court, creating an unforgettable sequence of masterpieces. His position as court painter led to an increasing formality and reticence of style. The touching human qualities to be found in his early work are absent, and Holbein's sitters confront us through the impressive attributes of status and power. Among his specifically royal portraits are those of Jane Seymour and Anne of Cleves (*Plates 45 and 47*), two of Henry's misfortunate queens, and that of the young Prince Edward (*Plate 52*), later Edward VI, painted as a new year's gift from the artist (1539/40). Even here, in the portrait of a two-year-old, Holbein conveys a dignity and solemnity appropriate to a great personage. The importance attached to a male heir is underlined by the lines of verse which appear on the portrait in praise of Henry and his dynasty.

Many of Henry's matrimonial and political problems had been created by his need to secure the succession. Edward's birth in 1537 was greeted with profound relief, though tempered by the knowledge that he was physically frail. Fears of what might happen after Henry's death continued to haunt the minds of Tudor statesmen. They were accentuated by growing religious divisions within the country and the threat of intervention from outside. The picture of *Edward VI and the Pope* (*Plate 49*) is primarily an anti-papal satire, but it also stresses the need for political continuity. Henry VIII, on his death-bed, points to Edward and his council as if beseeching loyalty to his son and heir. The theme of the Protestant succession is the subject of a later allegory, *The family of Henry VIII* (*Plate 48*), painted in the 1570s. Seated on a throne, Henry VIII entrusts the sword of justice to his son, Edward VI. His elder daughter, Mary I, stands on the left with her husband, Philip II, and Mars, the god of war. Henry's younger daughter, Elizabeth I, is shown on the right trampling discord underfoot, and pointing to Peace and Plenty, who attend her. Another pictorial demonstration of Elizabeth's virtue is the strange allegory at Hampton Court (*Plate 51*), in which she confounds the three goddesses and awards the golden apple to herself. She, too, appears in anti-papal satires, like the Dutch print reproduced here (*Plate 50*), in which she exposes the hypocrisy and corruption of the Roman Church.

As Prince of Wales, Edward VI was much portrayed, but there is only one recorded portrait type of him as king (*Plate 53*). This shows him in doublet and hose, posed before a setting of classical architecture, and is probably the work of William Scrots, who succeeded Holbein as king's painter. Scrots had been employed at the court of Mary of Hungary in Brussels, and he brought with him the latest European court style. Nevertheless, the placing of Edward's figure, legs astride, clearly goes back to Holbein's wall painting, and shows the persistence of a pose now firmly associated with the person of the king. Like the Holbein of Henry VIII, the portrait of Edward was widely copied and circulated.

Few English portraitists of the mid sixteenth century are known by name, and foreign-born artists continued to enjoy the patronage of the court. The portrait of Edward's half-sister and successor, Mary I, by Anthonis Mor (*Plates 54 and 55*), one of three autograph versions, is an outstanding masterpiece, a living presence and a penetrating study of character. A contemporary described Mary's appearance as 'very grave. Her eyes are so piercing that they inspire, not only respect but fear . . . . In short she is a seemly person and never to be loathed for ugliness, even at her present age, without considering her degree of queen.' Mor is said to have been sent to England by the Emperor Charles V to paint Mary for her prospective bridegroom, Philip II of Spain, and to have been rewarded with a golden chain and a pension. His visit to England is not recorded, and it was, in any case, an isolated event. The dominant artist at Mary's court was the intriguing and elusive Hans Eworth, who painted a number of generally small and intimate portraits of the queen, which present her in a sympathetic light. Eworth seems to have fallen from favour under Elizabeth, although he was employed as a designer for the series of fêtes put on for the French commissioners in 1572.

Mor's portrait of Mary gives us a fairly good idea of what she really looked like. One will search in vain for such a realistic representation of her successor. In almost none of the countless portraits of Elizabeth I do we sense a figure of flesh and blood. The face is like a mask, frozen and impenetrable, the body imprisoned in fantastically jewelled costumes. As images of state, Elizabeth's portraits give an overwhelming impression of splendour and magnificence. Their symbolism mirrors the elaborate mythology built up around the person of the queen. We see in visual form her attributes and virtues as extolled by the poets and writers of her court. To them she is a most high, mighty and magnificent empress, renowned for her piety, virtue and good government; the guardian of justice, peace and true religion; the chaste virgin and the mother of her people. At times her portraits take on the character of sacred images, and, if this seems sacrilegious, one must remember that in the post-Reformation age the Crown was the one symbol of national unity, to which people of every religious persuasion could subscribe.

The portraits of Elizabeth are only an extreme example of tendencies general to Elizabethan art. Isolated from the main centres of Europe by the confrontation between Protestants and Catholics, English painters evolved their own idiom, at once highly stylized and archaic. They turned their back on the tradition of Renaissance realism to create what Roy Strong calls 'the two-dimensional, bright, flower-coloured world of the high-Elizabethan portrait' (*The English Icon*, 1969). Symbolic and literary allusions abound in this splendidly decorative but strangely airless and introverted world. One has a feeling of secretiveness and mystification in the play of line and pattern, and one must not look here for revelations of appearance or character.

Elizabeth herself was highly sensitive about her appearance, and her influence and that of her court probably played a part in prolonging an essentially reactionary style. A draft proclamation of 1563 forbids the production of images of the queen, until such time as an official portrait has been approved as a pattern for artists to follow. Later in the reign, the Privy Council was seeking to suppress unauthorized portraits of Elizabeth, and to give the sergeant painter a censorship role. There were complaints, too, from the Painter Stainers Company, which hoped to preserve its monopoly, about untrained artists 'counterfeyting' her majesty's picture, from which we may conclude that the production of the royal image was a flourishing industry.

Most of the surviving portraits of Elizabeth can be related to one of a number of limited face patterns. It is clear that they were not the property of any one studio, but circulated freely, possibly in the form of drawings. The chronology of these face patterns does not always reflect the changing appearance of the queen. The famous '*Rainbow portrait*' (*Plate 57*), which can be dated on costume to around 1600, makes use of a face pattern developed over twenty years earlier.

Elizabeth seems to have been reluctant to give sittings, and only five artists are recorded as having painted her, presumably in most cases from life. Roy Strong in his study of her portraits lists a further three artists who may have done so. There is one marvellous portrait of Elizabeth as a princess (*Plate 56*), now tentatively attributed to Scrots, but the portraits produced during the early years of her reign are few in number and disappointing in quality. It is not till the 1570s that the great output of royal images begins, coinciding with a renaissance of the arts in general. Four portraits of very high quality, dating from about 1575–80, reflect the influence of Nicholas Hilliard, who entered royal service at that period, while the well-known '*Darnley portrait*' (National Portrait Gallery) is more continental in style.

Hilliard was a miniaturist, and no certain larger scale painting by him is known, but he is the dominant figure in the development of an esoteric court style in the late Elizabethan period. In his treatise on limning or miniature painting, Hilliard records that the queen insisted on being painted out of doors in full sunlight, 'where no tree was neere, nor anye shadow at all'. His miniatures mark the apotheosis of the bright, shadowless world of Elizabethan portraiture, with its arabesque patterns and vivid, heraldic colour. His first miniature of Elizabeth is dated 1572 (*Plate 60*), and he continued to paint her until the end of the reign, his portraits becoming ever more fantastic and elaborate (*Plate 62*). After such stylized creations as these, it comes as something of a shock to be confronted with Isaac Oliver's naturalistic portrayal of Elizabeth (*Plate 61*). The veil of illusion is temporarily cast aside for a rare glimpse of the ageing queen. The circumstances in which Oliver came to paint the miniature are unknown, and we can only speculate on the reasons why it remained unfinished.

The official portraits of Elizabeth in the last years of her reign are essentially cult objects. Around 1588 a new face pattern emerges, associated with a series of portraits produced at the time of the Armada. Elizabeth is depicted in triumph, her hand resting on a globe, symbol of supremacy at sea and world empire, while scenes of the naval battle are shown in the background (*Plate 58*). In William Rogers's engraving (*Plate 63*), she is praised as 'Th' admired Empresse through the worlde applauded', and the emblems of pelican and phoenix, shown on either side, refer to her role as mother of her people and the promised imperial virgin. The glorification of monarchy is carried still further in the full-length '*Ditchley portrait*' by Gheeraerts in the National Portrait Gallery, where she floats goddess-like above a map of England. A sonnet in a cartouche hails her as the 'prince of light', and in the background shafts of sunlight disperse the stormy clouds.

The Stuarts

The portraits of Elizabeth are part of the legend of a remarkable queen, whose reign has always seemed like a golden age. In the more prosaic atmosphere of James I's court, the highly-charged elements of Elizabethan imagery evaporated. The dominant artists were Anglo-Flemish, and they brought English painting back into line with naturalistic trends on the Continent. As far as royal portraiture went, the result was a decided lowering in visual temperature. James I, who was not much interested in the arts, disliked sitting for his portrait. The earliest type showing him as king is associated with John de Critz (*Plate 64*); certainly a more realistic representation than any of the portraits of Elizabeth, but it is banal by comparison. James's appearance was not prepossessing. He is described by a contemporary as a man of 'timorous disposition, which was the reason of his quilted doublets, his eye large, ever rowling after any stranger came in his presence . . . his Beard was very thin . . . his legs were very weak . . . his walk was ever circular'. James was not much better served by other artists in his service. Hilliard was well past his best (*Plate 65*), and Van Somer, who replaced de Critz, painted a very routine state portrait of the king in 1618 (Royal Collection). The most moving image of James in later life is the seated portrait by Daniel Mytens (National Portrait Gallery), in which he is shown loaded down by his garter robes, looking old and worn.

It was left to James's queen, Anne of Denmark, and to his son, Henry, Prince of Wales, to promote new tastes and styles. Henry was in the forefront of artistic developments, in architecture, painting, collecting and the staging of masques. Theatricals were a passion with his mother as well. The early painting of him in the hunting field with a friend by Robert Peake (*Plate 69*) is an entirely new type of royal image. Hunting has always been regarded as one of the most important of princely accomplishments, but it had never before been the subject of a state portrait. A series of later royal hunting scenes derive from this rather primitive work, with its stiff figures and stagey landscape. Among the earliest examples are the full-length portrait of Anne of Denmark by Van Somer (Royal Collection) walking in hunting clothes through a sombre landscape; Daniel Mytens's group of Charles I and Henrietta Maria departing for the chase (*Plate 72*); and Van Dyck's picture of Charles I dressed *à la chasse* in the Louvre, the masterpiece of the genre.

Equally original as a royal image is the heroic picture of Prince Henry on horseback, now at Parham Park, a predecessor of Van Dyck's equestrian portraits of Charles I (*Plate 75*). Isaac Oliver, the miniaturist, has plausibly been suggested as the artist, although, as in the case of Hilliard, no life-size paintings by him have as yet been documented. He had succeeded Peake in the prince's service, and his miniatures of Henry and Anne of Denmark (*Plate 67*) breathe a new spirit of elegant naturalism. Further light is thrown on the direction of Henry's taste by his efforts to lure the Dutch painter, Michael van Miereveldt, to his court. The arrival of such a distinguished and fashionable artist would certainly have altered the artistic situation in England, as Van Dyck's arrival was to do some twenty years later, but this, like other promising developments, was cut short by the prince's early death in 1612.

Prince Henry's artistic tastes were inherited by his younger brother, Charles I, whose reign marks one of the high-points in the history of royal portraiture. Charles's court was highly cultivated and refined, and, like that of Elizabeth, it indulged in an elaborate mythology of kingship. In the masques of the time, Charles is glorified as emperor and hero, the source of wisdom and true religion, while his French wife, Henrietta Maria, inspired a Platonic cult of courtly love. This framework of allegory, so dear to the seventeenth-century mind, finds expression in visual as well as literary form.

The portraits of Charles I present him in a variety of guises, as figure of majesty and imperial power, as courtly gallant and huntsman, and even, in a fanciful picture by Rubens (Royal Collection), as St George rescuing the princess in the person of his wife. The marriage of the royal couple was the subject of constant eulogy, symbolizing the unity of the state and the prosperity of Charles's rule. In Mytens's hunting group of about 1630–2

(*Plate 72*), we see Charles and Henrietta Maria tenderly holding hands, while a putto above showers them with roses, symbol of love. In a half-length double portrait by the same artist (Royal Collection), Henrietta bestows the victor's laurels on her husband, while holding a sprig of olive as a token of peace. The laurel and olive occur again in Hendrik Pot's charming conversation piece of the royal couple with their eldest child (Royal Collection), this time symbolizing the warlike virtues of Henrietta's father, Henry IV of France, and the peace-loving nature of Charles's father, James I.

In 1629, Charles commissioned a ceiling from Sir Peter Paul Rubens, to celebrate the achievements of his father, for Inigo Jones's recently built Banqueting Hall in Whitehall. The ceiling is not only a baroque masterpiece, but the most complete and powerful exposition of Stuart claims to absolute monarchy ever propagated in pictorial form. It is not surprising that Charles tried to secure Rubens as his court painter. He failed, but within two years he had landed almost as big a prize in the person of Sir Anthony van Dyck. The latter had originally trained in Rubens's studio, later establishing a European reputation as a court portraitist. He arrived in London (probably in March 1632) to be fêted, knighted and given a generous pension. During the remaining nine years of his life, Van Dyck painted some of the greatest and most persuasive royal portraits ever produced. His portraits of Charles I express the ideology of kingship in terms that are certainly formal, and often grand, but softened by virtue of his subtle technique. In the earliest royal commission (Royal Collection), Charles is shown with his wife and eldest children in an impressive architectural setting—the father of a family, and by analogy the father of his people. In the first of two equestrian portraits (*Plate 75*), he rides in triumph through a classical arch attended by his master of the horse, Monseigneur de Saint Antoine. Like the family group, this picture was intended to be viewed at the end of a long perspective formed by one of the galleries in St James's Palace. So powerfully illusionistic is the design that it must have seemed to the spectator as if Charles himself was riding in majesty down the gallery. The vitality of the horse and figures is echoed in the swirling draperies that frame the archway, and in the stormy sky behind. Apart from Charles himself, Van Dyck painted some ravishing portraits of Henrietta Maria (*Plate 76*), and some endearing groups of their children (*Plate 74*).

Van Dyck's portraits of the king provide an index to the types of state portrait current in England for the next hundred years or so. There are full-lengths in coronation robes and armour, three-quarter-lengths in armour and garter robes, the great equestrian portrait in the National Gallery, and the supremely elegant and elegaic picture of Charles in hunting costume in the Louvre. More informal, but no less dignified, is the famous triple portrait (*Plates 82 and 83*), painted to assist the Roman sculptor, Bernini, in his bust of the king. It is of the essence of Van Dyck's genius that he should convey not only the majesty of his subject, but the human individual as well. The features are refined and rather long drawn out, framed by fashionably long hair and by an elegant beard in the French manner. Charles has an air of immense dignity and self-possession, but he is also wistful, sensitive, withdrawn. Amidst the trappings of state, he seems preoccupied with some inner vision. Commentators then and since have read into his sad-eyed expression a premonition of the disaster that was to overwhelm him. This is a case of romantic hindsight, but it is none the less attractive for all that.

Van Dyck's sensitive interpretation of Charles's character and appearance has stamped itself on posterity. Portraits of the king by other artists look prosaic in comparison, but they tell another story. Honthorst's study of him reading (*Plate 73*), the first genuinely informal royal portrait, shows a smiling countenance. Geniality and good nature radiate from the early portraits by Daniel Mytens, Van Dyck's predecessor. In sculpture, too, we see a conventional interpretation of the king's face. The period is notable for the revival of this art form in England, and from now on it begins to play a significant role in state portraiture. The most famous sculpture of Charles I is the imposing bronze equestrian statue that stands at the top of Whitehall by the French artist, Hubert Le Sueur (*Plate 81*). He was responsible for reintroducing bronze as a medium, and for establishing in this country the independent portrait bust. Other sculptors employed by the court include Francesco Fanelli and François Dusart, the latter responsible for a fine marble bust of 1636 (*Plate 80*). The outstanding sculpture of Charles is unfortunately lost—the famous marble bust by Bernini, for which Van Dyck painted his triple portrait. From the evidence of copies, it must have been a work of great power and virtuosity. Thomas Chambers, who transported it from Rome, wrote 'of the astonishment of the whole court, in particular of the superintendent of the statues, who exclaimed with an oath as the first plank of the case was raised that the bust is a miracle'.

The portraits of Charles so far discussed date from the period of his personal rule. From 1629 to 1640 no parliament was summoned, and it seemed as if Charles's attempt to establish absolute power might succeed. The brilliance of his court was a reflection of his statecraft. Artists and architects, musicians and dramatists, poets and philosophers, gathered to celebrate his achievements. With the advent of civil war all this came to an end. Significantly no new portraits of Charles were executed during the course of the war, although the demand for popular prints and woodcuts of him intensified. Portraiture, like other arts, does not flourish during periods of crisis.

After his defeat, Charles was recorded on at least three occasions. Most of the miniatures of him as king are after oil paintings, but the portrait by John Hoskins, dating from around 1645 (versions at Windsor and the Rijksmuseum, Amsterdam), appears to be from life. Hoskins was the leading miniaturist of the period and the quality of his work can be judged from the exquisite miniature of Henrietta Maria (*Plate 78*). The miniature of the king shows him simply dressed, with no symbol of rank apart from the garter, looking drawn and careworn. In Lely's portrait of him with his son, James, Duke of York (*Plate 84*), he has become a figure of tragic nobility. The last recorded portrait of Charles is by Edward Bower (*Plate 85*), showing him at the time of his trial. Four signed versions of the portrait are known, and it has been suggested that the slight differences in the arrangement of the hands and accessories in each of them represent various characteristic gestures observed by the artist.

Charles's execution in 1649 had a traumatic effect throughout Europe. It is difficult now to appreciate the mystique that then attached to the person of the king, both as the head of the Church and the embodiment of the state. The event itself was recorded in several crude woodcuts, which gained wide currency in England and abroad (*Plate 86*). At the same time, royal apologists began propagating the cult of the martyred king. In William Marshall's engraving at the front of *Eikon Basilike*, a book about the king's misfortunes (*Plate 87*), Charles is shown rejecting the temporal crown for a celestial diadem and a crown of thorns. Analogies between Charles's execution and Christ's Passion were frequently invoked, and Charles achieved his apotheosis both as Christian martyr and royalist hero.

The restoration of the monarchy in 1660 was accompanied by an unprecedented outburst of popular support. The repressive nature of the Puritan regime, and the political vacuum following Cromwell's death in 1658, had created a mood of uncertainty and disillusionment. Charles II represented the promise of liberation and stability, and he ascended the throne in an atmosphere of almost universal rejoicing. It is possible to recapture this mood of excitement in the many paintings and engravings that record Charles's last days in exile and his journey to London (*Plate 88*). One of the most delightful is the picture by Hieronymus Janssens, recording a ball at The Hague (*Plate 89*), where Charles's pleasure in the entertainments of court life is very evident. Later conversation pieces in a similar vein depict Charles walking outside Whitehall Palace, attending the races, leaving Hampton Court in his coach, and, as a patron of horticulture, receiving a pineapple from the royal gardener (*Plate 93*). These paintings, presenting charming and informal scenes of royal life, are far more satisfying than the pompous allegories perpetrated by foreign artists like Antonio Verrio.

If, in the popular mind, the accession of Charles II, Charles I's eldest son, looked like the dawn of a new age, to the royalists it meant the restoration of the old order. The famous oak tree in which Charles had hidden, during his escape from England after the Battle of Worcester in 1650, had been taken up by his followers as the symbol of an indestructible monarchy, sanctioned by immemorial tradition and divine right. Charles himself toyed with the idea of establishing an order of the royal oak, and it is no coincidence that he is shown with a wreath of oak leaves in his hair in the early coins and medallions by Thomas Simon and John Roettier.

But, if the restoration of 1660 looked superficially like a return to the old regime, the reality was very different. Although the externals of monarchy might appear to be the same, the substance was lacking. True, everything still revolved around the court, and that at least seemed as impressive and glamorous as ever, but the fundamental ideology had gone. Charles I had believed in his role as an absolute monarch, a divinely appointed agent of God. For all his shifts and subterfuges, Charles II remained to the end a constitutional monarch.

It is doubtful if a great state portrait can be produced without the stimulus of a noble idea of what constitutes the essence of monarchy. Sir Peter Lely, Charles II's court painter, was of course no Van Dyck. His only autograph portrait of his royal patron (*Plate 94*) shows him in garter robes, seated on a dais with the regalia beside him. The attitude of the figure is natural and lively, and the sardonic features of the king are lit up with a look of intelligence and amusement. There is a baroque sumptuousness in the treatment of costume and accessories, the gilded throne, for example, with its exuberant curves and caryatid figures echoing the border of the tapestry and the richly brocaded table-cloth. As an image it is more relaxed and more florid than anything comparable by Van Dyck. But, whereas Van Dyck could reconcile ideal qualities of kingship with a profound feeling for the individual underneath, Lely's portrait retains an air of artifice, as if neither we nor the king were expected to take the thing too seriously.

Lely employed a large and efficient studio, and his output of royal portraits must have been considerable. At the time of his death in 1680, nineteen portraits of the king were recorded in his possession. A certain amount of confusion surrounds the different portrait types for which he was responsible, and the problem is not made easier by the fact that face patterns were exchanged between studios, as in Elizabethan times. Hence the ease with which similar portraits of the king are variously attributed to Lely and Huysmans, Lely and Wissing, and so forth. We have entered an era when the concept of the unique work of art has been all but submerged by the pressures of mass production. Portraits were no longer a luxury for a relatively small élite, but part of the furnishings of every decently appointed town or country house.

It is with some relief that one turns from the repetitive state portraits of Charles II to less conventional images. Outstanding among the early portraits of him are the miniatures by Samuel Cooper (*Plate 90*). They challenge comparison with large-scale portraiture in their breadth of effect and instinctive power of design. But Cooper scores over his rivals in large by his vivid perception of character. Under his robes of state, Charles II lives as an individual, and Cooper's miniatures of him have all the freshness of an original vision. The much later bust of Charles by the French sculptor, Honoré Pelle (*Plate 92*), captures one's attention for the same reason. Extravagance of style has replaced Cooper's restrained naturalism, but the bust, like the miniature, is vital and alive. In the best traditions of baroque sculpture, it combines elaborate detail with a theatrical sense of movement. The characterization borders on caricature, but how much more memorable it is than the painted stereotypes.

Charles II's brother, James II, ruled for too short a time to make much impact on the arts. There are many good portraits of him as Duke of York, and he was a collector and patron of some note. He sat to Samuel Cooper on several occasions (*Plate 95*), and from Lely he commissioned two important sets of portraits, the Flagmen, a group of naval commanders now at Greenwich, and the famous Windsor Beauties. Had he remained in power, and had he been permitted to carry through his plans for restoring Roman Catholicism and absolute rule, he would no doubt have promoted a more allegorical form of portraiture, in line with that of other Catholic monarchs. Already, by the beginning of his reign, he was collecting around him a group of foreign artists sympathetic to his aims. It was Antonio Verrio, an Italian artist noted for his mural decorations, who was appointed principal painter to James, not Lely's successors, William Riley or Godfrey Kneller. The latter had painted a distinguished full-length of James as lord high admiral in 1684 (*Plate 97*), but he painted no new portraits of the king after his accession. One artist who did was the Frenchman, Nicholas de Largillière, who was encouraged to return to London, from which, as a Catholic, he had been excluded by the passage of the Test Act a few years earlier. His portrait of the new king (*Plate 96*) has an air of continental refinement, and it is a matter for regret that his influence was so short-lived. He was a portraitist of high calibre, and his charming picture of the Old Pretender and his sister (National Portrait Gallery), painted in exile, is evidence of what he might have achieved if he had stayed in England after James's overthrow.

The Glorious Revolution of 1688, which replaced James II by his daughter, Mary II, and her husband, William III, merely confirmed the *status quo* so far as the arts were concerned. Sir Godfrey Kneller, who may have antagonized James II with his Whig connections, emerged triumphant, his rivals either dead or departed. Kneller's career, which spans five reigns, was one of unexampled success. He amassed a fortune, was created a baronet (the first artist to receive this honour before the late nineteenth century), and bought his way into the landed gentry. His first official portraits of William III and Mary II (Royal Collection) were executed soon after their coronation in 1691, from sittings apparently given the previous year. The portrait of William is not an original design, deriving from Van Dyck's portrait of Charles I in coronation robes, but it is a solid and distinguished piece of painting. Some idea of the rewards enjoyed by successful court painters can be gauged from the large number of copies of these two state portraits for which payments are recorded. Kneller was paid £500 on two occasions in 1693 for ten full-lengths of William and Mary, and, in the years immediately following, numerous additional copies were ordered, for ministers, ambassadors, foreign sovereigns and institutions of every kind, at the same price level. The production of the state portrait had become a highly organized and lucrative business.

William III sat to relatively few artists after his accession. The demands of strenuous military campaigning can have left him little time, and, unlike his rival, Louis XIV of France, he was not personally vain. Kneller's great equestrian picture of the king (Royal Collection), painted to celebrate the successful negotiations leading to the Peace of Ryswick in 1697, makes use of the same face pattern as the earlier coronation portrait. It is a grandiose design, rooted in the conventions of baroque allegory, with figures and emblems symbolic of peace and plenty, martial triumph and imperial power. A number of other equestrian portraits, showing William on the battlefield (the Battle of the Boyne was a favourite scene), are associated with Jan Wyck and his school. They are derivative as portraits and mostly mechanical in quality. Schalcken's unusual candlelight portrait (*Plate 98*) is said to have been painted from life, but its close dependence on Kneller's face pattern makes this unlikely. Apart from Kneller, the only artists who seem to have received sittings were sculptors: Cavalier for his medallion of 1690 in the Victoria and Albert Museum; Blommendael for the bust executed in The Hague in 1699 (*Plate 99*); and the modeller of the wax effigy in Westminster Abbey (*Plate 100*), almost certainly based on a death mask. This last portrait reveals the gaunt structure of William's head, the furrowed cheeks and large, hooked nose. It is a timeless image of the individual, stripped of all pomp and circumstance.

The portraits of Mary II and her sister, Anne, seem rather characterless by comparison with those of William III. Indeed, it is significant that the early portraits of the two sisters have often been confused. Portraits of ladies at this period tend to conform to a limited number of types, and they aspire to a generalized ideal of feminine beauty. The introduction of state robes and regalia adds a new element to portraits of otherwise fashionable ladies, but conveys no stronger sense of individual distinction. The standard coronation portrait of Mary by Kneller has already been discussed. The first state portrait of Anne is also by Kneller, a stiff and rather hieratic image showing her standing; there is also a seated version. He later painted some less formal, more feminine portraits, including one in profile for the coinage. Anne also sat to Kneller's chief rival, the Swedish painter, Michael Dahl, and to the obscure Edmund Lilly (*Plate 102*). She appears in several allegorical decorations by Verrio at Hampton Court, and in a sketch for a projected picture by Kneller, showing her presenting the plans of Blenheim to the Duke and Duchess of Marlborough (Blenheim Palace). A guide to her popularity is provided by the relatively large number of statues erected in her honour. Francis Bird sculpted several during her lifetime, the most famous of which stood for many years in front of St Paul's (replaced now by a nineteenth-century copy), and there are posthumous examples by Rysbrack and others.

The Hanoverians

Royal portraiture reaches a low ebb during the early years of the eighteenth century. George I and George II, Anne's Hanoverian cousins and successors, were both extraordinarily philistine, and they cared almost nothing about the arts. In the past, the court had been the centre of artistic patronage, promoting the latest styles, and employing the most talented artists of the day. The eighteenth century witnessed an unparalleled flowering of the arts in Great Britain, but most of this activity took place outside and without reference to the court. Patronage was now in the hands of the great landed aristocrats, whose country mansions reflected the taste and wealth of the new age.

Both early Georges seem to have regarded their portraits with indifference, and, as they sat to some of the dullest painters of the period, the results are predictably mediocre. Kneller's coronation portrait of George I, and his official portrait of George II as Prince of Wales, are very similar in design, and they were both borrowed from a pattern much used by Kneller's studio. That of George I is said to have been the only one for which he gave sittings, and portraits of him by other artists seem to depend on Kneller's image (*see Plate 103*). He and his family are represented in the fine baroque decoration of the Painted Hall at Greenwich by Sir James Thornhill and Dietrich André, celebrating the Hanoverian succession, but the quality of portraiture is unfortunately marred by coarse execution. Among the most elegant portraits of the king are the busts by Rysbrack, one of which is reproduced (*Plate 104*).

The situation was no better during the reign of George II, whose relations with artists were not happy. The coronation portraits of himself and his wife, Caroline of Ansbach, by Charles Jervas resemble stuffed dummies, and they are said to have cost the artist much 'favour & Interest at Court'. A project for a royal conversation piece by Hogarth was thwarted by his rival, William Kent, and the indifference of the king. Later portraits of George II were usually painted without the benefit of sittings. The seated full-length of 1744 by Thomas Hudson (National Portrait Gallery) is a competent work, but, according to George Vertue, 'His Majesty did not honour him to set purposely for it'. The same is true of the marble bust by Roubiliac (*Plate 108*), the most distinguished piece of royal sculpture since Bernini's bust of

Charles I. It is possible that John Shackleton, principal painter from 1749, received sittings for his portrait of George in the Foundling Hospital (*Plate 106*), but it is unlikely that Thomas Worlidge or Richard Edge Pine had the same good fortune. Worlidge produced a striking profile portrait of the king, and Pine's brilliantly vivid sketch, now at Audley End, Essex, is almost a caricature. George II was a good subject for satirical treatment, as George Townshend, the first royal caricaturist, had discovered (*Plate 107*). 'He is of a delicate build', wrote a contemporary, 'and has a fine foot and shows it off like a coquette. He holds himself in a particularly erect fashion, that his courtiers call majestic. His features are also peculiar, protuberant blue eyes, a fine nose and a big mouth, not unlike the crescent moon.'

As in the reign of James I, the arts found their champion not in the person of the king but of the Prince of Wales. Like his predecessor, Prince Henry, Frederick, Prince of Wales, was a lavish and discerning patron of contemporary art, and a great collector. His father, whose chief interest was the army, was irritated by the aesthetic and intellectual outlook of his son, and they were constantly at loggerheads. While George II was refusing to sit to artists, Frederick sat all the time to the leading talents of the day. Early on he employed the French painter, Philip Mercier, who had studied with Watteau, and Mercier's conversation piece of the prince and his sisters playing music (*Plate 105*), with its charming air of informality and its pastoral setting, is conceived in the spirit of French rococo art. This is the first genuinely off-duty glimpse of the royal family, pursuing a hobby. Frederick and his sisters were keen amateur musicians and discerning connoisseurs of contemporary music.

Through his patronage, Frederick was helping to promote new forms of art, and he stamped his personality firmly on the works which he commissioned. There are, for example, a highly important group of hunting pictures of the prince and his friends by John Wootton, one of them painted with the assistance of Hogarth. Hunting had been a theme of royal portraiture since the early seventeenth century, but Wootton's figures are not self-consciously posed, but arrange themselves naturally across the picture space as elements in a landscape. Frederick introduced new themes and motifs to royal portraiture in the elegant group of his wife, Princess Augusta, with her family and household, and in the charming picture by Barthélemy du Pan of his children playing in the gardens of Park Place (both Royal Collection). Portraits of Frederick himself by Amigoni, Highmore and Van Loo have more style and animation than any royal portraits painted since the seventeenth century. There is a warmth of feeling in the characterizations of this amiable and cultivated prince that communicates itself strongly. With his pronounced Hanoverian features, large mouth and bulging eyes, he was scarcely handsome, but infinitely more engaging as a personality than either his father or his grandfather.

Frederick did not live to inherit the throne, but the atmosphere of taste which he had created left its mark. His son, George III, who became king in 1760 on the death of George II, was well aware of the importance of the arts. If he lacked Frederick's instinctive flair and enthusiasm, he made up for this by doing what he considered to be his duty. His greatest single act was to sanction the foundation of the Royal Academy in 1768, and he took an active interest in the affairs of that institution. Throughout his reign he commissioned works from contemporary artists, chiefly portraits, for he was the devoted father of a large family, and liked to record those who were dear to him. The royal conversation piece, pioneered by Frederick, was encouraged by George III. He must have admired the realistic style of the German painter, Johann Zoffany, for he commissioned him to paint a succession of royal groups. There can be few more enchanting family pictures than that of Queen Charlotte sitting by her dressing table in Buckingham Palace, with her two eldest sons (*Plate 113*). There is a feeling of radiant early morning in this informal scene, with its vivid colouring and wealth of descriptive detail.

For all his efforts on behalf of the arts, George III does not seem to have had much of an eye for quality. He disliked Reynolds, and only employed Gainsborough late in that artist's career. The appointment of the Scottish artist, Allan Ramsay, as his principal painter seems to have been due to the influence of his close friend, Lord Bute, rather than to any strong personal predeliction. Bute had commissioned from Ramsay, whose patron he was, a strikingly original full-length of George III shortly before his accession. With the advent of the new reign, the king naturally chose Ramsay, one of the few artists whom he knew, for the coronation portrait. Ramsay also executed a profile study of George for the coinage (*Plate 110*).

The choice of Ramsay was a fortunate one. The powerful naturalism of his early style had been refined through contact with continental art. His state portrait of George III (*Plate 109*) is a *tour de force*. The elegantly turned figure of the king in a gold suit is set off by luxuriant ermine robes and a great looped curtain behind. The sense of movement and the brilliant powdered colour seem to have their source in French rococo art. But Ramsay's conception is solider and less theatrical than comparable portraits of Louis XV, conveying the dignified character of the young king with sensitivity. After the repetitive state portraits of his predecessors, Ramsay's picture of George III has all the freshness and life of an original conception, and it remains one of the greatest of English royal portraits. It is also one of the best known. Ramsay established a special studio of assistants to cope with the enormous demand for copies of this portrait and a companion piece of Queen Charlotte.

Later state portraits of George are dull in comparison with the Ramsay. It is the Gainsborough of Queen Charlotte (Royal Collection) that one remembers for its brilliance of handling. Lawrence's portrait of her in old age

(National Gallery) is a masterpiece, but there is nothing comparable of her husband, although he sat to Reynolds and West, Lawrence and Beechey. His character was rather ordinary, and he inspired no great works of art.

That he inspired affection can be shown by the large number of popular images of him that survive in various mediums. His simple, unaffected manners appealed to his fellow countrymen, and there was a constant demand for his likeness. This was the age of the cheap print, and there were new forms of popular portraiture, like the silhouette and the portrait wax, both of which the royal couple helped to promote. It was also the age of the satirical print and the caricature. George Townshend was apparently the first artist to poke fun at the royal family in his drawings of George II (*Plate 107*). By the end of the century, the Crown had become the target for savage attacks by artists like Gillray and Cruikshank. The dissolute and extravagant Prince of Wales was especially vulnerable, and his reputation has never escaped from the ridicule heaped on him by Gillray (*Plate 114*). Many of Gillray's caricatures border on the obscene and libellous, but the eighteenth century was less squeamish about character assassination than we are today.

George IV can be forgiven much, for underneath the profligate and showman was a man of taste and an ardent collector. With Henry VIII and Charles I, he deserves to rank as one of the greatest of royal patrons. Not only did he commission works from artists of the day, but he helped to create the distinctive style of decoration, the Regency, that takes its name from his title as Prince Regent. The houses that he lived in he either rebuilt or redesigned, commissioning splendid and beautiful interiors as a setting for his large collection of works of art. Schemes of decoration were thought through comprehensively as part of a luxurious and aesthetic style of life. The people surrounding the Prince of Wales were as careless and improvident as himself, a veritable galaxy of wit and talent, and it is not surprising that his debts reached astronomical proportions. But nothing could restrain him from continuing to lavish money on the arts, which satisfied both his love of display and his deep creative instincts. The Brighton Pavilion, a mixture of folly and extravaganza, is a tribute to the originality of his taste.

Flamboyant and good-looking as a young man, with a passion for dressing-up, George IV was an admirable subject for portraiture. Artists responded to his personality, and most of the likenesses of him as Prince of Wales are vivid and attractive. He is often depicted in romantic surroundings, his face alive with expression. Even in the most formal portraits of him, like the grandiose Reynolds of 1787 (*Plate 115*), his exuberant personality comes across strongly. The design is full of movement and vitality, the negro attendant in hussar uniform stepping across to secure the prince's magnificent garter robes, as he half turns away. Unlike his father, George IV admired Reynolds, and he sat to him for a second dramatic full-length with charger. Gainsborough painted him on several occasions, as did John Hoppner (his principal painter from 1793), Sir William Beechey, Richard Brompton, John Russell, and, in the medium of miniature and drawing, his early favourite, Richard Cosway.

The advent of the Regency in 1811, as a result of George III's mental breakdown, coincided with the Prince Regent's patronage of Sir Thomas Lawrence, the greatest portrait painter of the age. Lawrence had painted George III as early as 1792, and he had been appointed principal painter in succession to Reynolds in the same year. Though he had been promised sittings by the prince in 1804, he had to wait another ten years before securing a commission; a delay for which his close friendship with the prince's estranged wife, Caroline (*Plate 117*), may have been responsible. Once introduced to Lawrence, the Prince Regent responded to his genius and charm, and he proceeded to commission a set of portraits of the allied sovereigns and commanders (now in the Waterloo Chamber at Windsor). The prince's confidence was not misplaced, for Lawrence painted some of his greatest works in the service of his royal patron. His first portrait of the prince himself is cast in the same heroic mould as the Waterloo portraits, showing him in the uniform of a field marshal, sword in hand, posed against a stormy sky (Marquess of Londonderry). The brilliant unfinished sketch of the Prince Regent in profile (*Plate 118*) dates from the same period. Around 1818 Lawrence painted him in garter robes, and later he adapted this design for the first official portrait of George IV as king (*Plate 116*), substituting coronation robes for those of the garter. Like the Ramsay of George III, the Lawrence of his successor is entirely original and contemporary in spirit. One is not conscious of the machinery of the state portrait, as one is in the work of more mundane artists. Lawrence convinces us that we see the real George IV before us, a figure swaggering and majestic but intensely alive. It needs a great artist to transcend the conventions of royal portraiture and to impose his own vision. Lawrence was a romantic, and his vision was far from objective. His contemporaries may be forgiven for failing to recognize the king in Lawrence's highly flattering portrait. To one who attended his coronation, George IV appeared very differently: 'Anybody who could have seen his disgusting figure with a wig the curls of which hung down his back, and quite bending beneath the weight of his robes and his sixty years would have been quite sick . . .'

The bluff and nautical Duke of Clarence, who succeeded his brother as William IV in 1830, had little interest in the arts. Lawrence, to whom he had sat before his accession (*Plate 120*), was dead, and he accepted his brother's choice of successor without demur. Sir David Wilkie had first made his name with minutely detailed scenes of Scottish life, two of them commissioned by George IV. He had gradually developed a broader manner of painting under the influence of the Italian masters. His portrait of William IV in uniform (*Plate 121*) lacks the panache of Lawrence, but the forms are strong, and a mood of drama is communicated by the play of light and dark. Suaver but less memorable is the portrait of William by Sir Martin Archer Shee, an artist brought up in the traditions of Georgian portraiture, and Lawrence's successor as president of the Royal Academy. William liked Shee's work so much that he insisted on keeping his portrait of Queen Adelaide (*Plate 122*), originally commissioned by the Goldsmiths Company. The artist records the difficulties he encountered with the subject, who 'particularly requests that the picture may not be flattered'.

Queen Victoria to the present day

The accession of William's niece, the eighteen-year-old Queen Victoria, in 1837 marks a significant turning-point in the history of royal portraiture. A new sensibility makes itself felt, and the range of imagery multiplies beyond all bounds. There were no more ardent advocates of Victorian taste than the young queen and the earnest, art-loving Prince Albert, whom she married in 1840. Not only did they patronize the leading painters of the Victorian school, but they established a vogue for totally new kinds of royal portrait. They were the parents of a large family, and occasions like births and marriages were commemorated in large formal groups. The artist was also invited behind the scenes to record informal incidents of family life in a manner unthinkable a generation or two earlier. Domesticity had become a royal virtue, linking the monarchy with the aspirations of ordinary men and women.

The number and variety of portraits and groups commissioned by Victoria and Albert was enormous, but it was nothing to the attention focused on them from outside. The growth of illustrated journalism and the advent of photography, not to speak of a vast print market, meant that images of the royal couple were constantly reproduced. The weight of visual documentation is overpowering, and it increased as the century went on. The queen's face must have been familiar to everyone, even in the lowest reaches of society. And not only her face, but the details of her public life. The woodcut artist and the photographer waited in the wings to record every important event or function for transmission to the public. Modern methods of reproduction and communication had transformed the whole basis of royal image making. The monarchy was still deeply entrenched in tradition, and the state portrait had an important part to play in preserving that tradition, but it stood now at the apex of a pyramid based on popular imagery. Queen Victoria endeared herself to her people as few other British monarchs have done, and the fact that she was a familiar, everyday figure and not a remote icon of majesty undoubtedly encouraged this sentiment.

The popular enthusiasm that greeted Victoria's accession in 1837 is reflected in the early portraits of her, no less than in the literary records of the time. Her youth and vitality stood in contrast to the elderly and unappealing characteristics of her predecessors. She sat to the portraitists employed by William IV, Shee and Wilkie, but she cordially hated the results. Her favourites were George Hayter, C. R. Leslie, Edwin Landseer and, a little later, Franz Winterhalter and Francis Grant. All of them responded to her gaiety and charm. In the well-known state portrait of her by Hayter, she is seated under an imposing canopy, weighed down by the crown and dalmatic robes. But, burdened as she is, she looks up with an expression of girlish eagerness and idealism. In Hayter's heroic coronation group (*Plate 123*), the first of its kind, we, like the spectators in the picture, are invited to acclaim the young and touchingly diminutive figure of the new queen. 'There was something pathetic, too, in her extreme youthfulness,' wrote a contemporary, 'her face had still the flush and flower-like look of childhood, from which, small and slim as she was, she might easily be supposed to have not yet emerged. . . . She had so much natural dignity, and such an air of distinction.'

Hayter, the artist of the later wedding and christening groups, represents the world of official portraiture. Landseer, on the other hand, was the private artist, the friend and confidant of the royal couple, and the teacher who gave them lessons in drawing and etching. His earliest portrait of the queen is the tender oil sketch of her, almost in profile, which she gave to Prince Albert as a Christmas present in 1839. In the same year Landseer painted several spirited equestrian sketches of the queen, and began the series of pictures of royal pets for which he is famous. He made informal paintings and drawings of the children, and he executed a number of family groups, the most important of which is the work called *Windsor Castle in modern times* (*Plate 124*)—an image of domestic bliss in a romantic vein. The royal couple led the vogue for fancy-dress balls, and Landseer's picture of them as Edward III and Queen Philippa (*Plate 127*) epitomizes the contemporary taste for historical pageant and make-believe. The ball at Buckingham Palace was a domestic equivalent to the famous Eglington Tournament, a revival of a medieval entertainment, held in 1839. When Victoria and Albert discovered Scotland, Landseer went with them. Balmoral is full of his drawings and paintings of Scottish scenes, including pictures of the royal family on hill and loch. The tradition of the royal sporting picture takes on a new character in the picturesque setting of the Highlands.

Queen Victoria's favourite artist, apart from Landseer, was Franz Winterhalter, the German-born painter whose polished work and charming manners made him a favourite in many European courts. He had been introduced to Victoria by her uncle, Leopold of the Belgiums, and he was to carry out a vast number of royal commissions in England. His portraits of Victoria alone include two full-length state portraits (1843 and 1859), the most popular early portrait of her, a three-quarter-length (1842), two further full-lengths (1845 and 1850), two major group paintings connected with her visit to France in 1843 and the return visit of Louis-Philippe in 1844, the large family group of 1846, the strangely symbolical '*First of May*' (*Plate 130*), not to speak of a large range of informal works, including another delightful fancy-dress picture of her and Albert (*Plate 125*). Winterhalter's study of Victoria with unbraided hair (*Plate 128*) is a vivid and scintillating piece of painting, and one can understand why it remained Albert's favourite picture of his wife. Winterhalter painted other royal ladies for their husbands in the same tender and sensual style, the Empress Elizabeth of Austria, for example, painted, as it might be, in her boudoir in a state of undress.

Winterhalter's place was taken by another German artist, Heinrich von Angeli (*see Plate 133*), recommended by the queen's eldest daughter, Vicky, the Princess Royal, now married to the Crown Prince of Prussia. But after Albert's death in 1861, Victoria grew less interested in the arts, and the quality of royal portraiture declines. The process can be studied in the royal wedding groups. The commissions for the marriage groups of the Princess Royal and the Prince of Wales (1858 and 1863, respectively) went to first-rate artists, John Phillip and W. P. Frith, and both produced strikingly original and successful works. Commissions for the marriage pictures of Queen Victoria's younger children went to a series of nonentities, many of them foreign, G. H. Thomas, N. Chevalier, C. Magnussen, S. P. Hall and R. Caton Woodville. One of the few artists of any calibre to be employed was J. D. Linton, and negotiations over his commission for the marriage of the Duke of Albany (1882) reveal that the queen's chief concern was to get the largest number of figures included for the smallest possible price. Laurits Tuxen, a Danish artist, painted two wedding groups of Victoria's grandchildren, and the official Jubilee picture of the royal family in 1887 (*Plate 136*), a splendid piece of social documentation and surprisingly well painted. It is interesting to notice that twentieth-century group photographs look scarcely any less formal and artificial (*Plates 165 and 166*). Indeed the distinction between painting and photography becomes increasingly blurred where imagery is concerned. Sir W. Q. Orchardson's *The four generations* of 1897 (Carlton House Terrace) exploits a dynastic theme already popularized by the camera (*Plate 137*).

Queen Victoria was a photogenic subject, and it is the photographs of her that one remembers. Where the painters offer us a highly flattering impression of the queen's appearance, the camera records her glum expression and dumpy figure without subterfuge of any kind. The gap between ideal and reality is very evident. But reality, while revealing that she was no beauty, communicates a force of character far more effectively than the facile gloss of the artist.

Queen Victoria recognized the power of the camera. She enjoyed sitting to photographers, took a keen interest in the results, and constantly sent prints of herself to friends. The earliest recorded photograph of herself is a calotype of about 1844–5 (*Plate 129*), probably by Henry Collen, who was miniature painter to the queen and an early photographic pioneer. In the early 1850s, Roger Fenton captured family life at Windsor Castle in a brilliant series of photographs, direct, informal and yet carefully stage-managed. The example shown here (*Plate 131*) is artistic in composition and romantic in mood; Queen Victoria, dressed in a plaid, resembles a Highland mother protecting her brood. Family groups proliferate from this period on, by Dr Becker, Caldesi, Bembridge, de Ros, Mayall (*Plate 132*), and many others, enveloping the monarchy in a totally new range of visual images. Some photographs are formal and reserved, others touching in their display of family feeling and affection. The camera moves out of doors to record gatherings on the terrace, children on horseback, passengers in the pony carriage, people on the lawn. Always prominent is the small, round figure of the queen herself, sometimes sovereign, sometimes hostess, sometimes devoted wife clinging to the arm of Prince Albert, sometimes the mother of a large family. She occupies the centre of the picture not only by right of place but by force of personality.

Queen Victoria was intensely emotional, and the death of Prince Albert in 1861 left her utterly prostrated with grief and loneliness. She decided to devote her life to perpetuating his memory, and the photographs taken in the years immediately following his death are an extraordinary testament to her obsession. Queen Victoria parades her grief in almost theatrical fashion, clasping her children to her and gazing soulfully at a marble bust or picture of her dead husband (*Plate 132*). Contrary to general belief, the Victorians had no inhibitions about displaying their feelings, especially where death was concerned. There is something moving as well as absurd in Victoria's formalized expression of intense personal suffering.

The imagery of the queen's later photographs takes its tone from her personality. Sitting by a spinning wheel or forlornly fondling a dog, she assumes her role as the Widow of Windsor. Later she emerged from seclusion to become a venerable and much-loved figurehead. The photographs of her as Empress of India, or those taken at the time of the Jubilee in 1887, show the queen's immense dignity and self-possession. She had become an indestructible symbol, as regal in her black dress and white veil as any of her great predecessors. Not all her photographs are couched in such formal terms. There are the inevitable family groups, showing her surrounded now by grandchildren and great grandchildren, the grandmother of Europe at the centre of a vast family network. Occasionally we see her involved in some activity, working at state papers, as in the charming and characterful photograph of her at Frogmore (*Plate 135*), breakfasting at Nice, or riding out in her donkey carriage. It needed a press photographer to catch her off guard, and we must be grateful to them for some of the rare glimpses of a smile.

Conservative by nature, the monarchy has had to adapt to an unprecedented rate of change in the twentieth century. The symbolic ideas behind its forms and ceremonies have lost much of their meaning, and the Crown, like other institutions, can no longer rely on the weight of tradition alone to support it. Its value, even as a figurehead, is open to question, and there have been no lack of critics accusing it of being an expensive anachronism. Historically the British have always felt a strong affection for the Crown and might be described as monarchical by nature. But sentiment alone does not explain the monarchy's extraordinary powers of survival. Its greatest strength has been its apolitical status. The monarchy has occasionally had to surmount a constitutional crisis, but it has not been involved in the day-to-day stresses of modern politics. Nor have the royal family withdrawn behind the barriers of court life, like so many continental monarchies, nor have they behaved aristocratically, snobbishly or frivolously. All recent monarchs have possessed to a greater or lesser degree the common touch, and their unselfish devotion to duty has earned them respect and admiration. In difficult times they have proved to be adaptable without loss of essential dignity.

The style of monarchy has altered radically in the last seventy years. Edward VII, for all his love of pleasure and ostentation, was a stickler for form, and he knew what he owed to his position. It is only by comparison with his mother, Queen Victoria, that he appears to have relaxed the rules. His son, George V, was a figure of great simplicity and integrity, whose love of sport and hatred of humbug made him popular with all ranks of society. He was the first king to make his voice heard to the nation through the medium of the radio, and the Christmas Broadcast became a firm tradition. George V's eldest son, Edward VIII, later Duke of Windsor, broke through the reserve surrounding the monarchy, by meeting people in a direct way. His concern with social problems led him to visit depressed areas to see for himself what conditions were like (*Plate 154*). This involvement with contemporary affairs was exemplified by the conduct of George VI and Queen Elizabeth during the Second World War (*Plates 160 and 161*). They made people feel that they were sharing a common experience, and they helped to keep morale high by displaying personal courage in the face of adversity. The present royal family have continued to bring the monarchy closer to the lives of ordinary people. They have travelled more widely in the United Kingdom, the Commonwealth and the world at large, than any of their predecessors. Royal affairs are less subject to censorship, and we have much more insight into their public and private lives than ever before.

The evolution of the monarchy is paralleled by a profound change in our way of visualizing it. Few people could name a single state portrait painted within the last seventy years. This is not just a reflection on the sorry state of traditional portraiture but an indication of a shift in emphasis. Our visual appetites are gargantuan, and we are no longer satisfied with the single composite picture. We build up an impression of the personality and appearance of someone well-known through a succession of images, presented either in photographic or film form. The process is complex and also repetitious, especially where royalty are concerned. We see them so often that it is impossible to pinpoint any particular image that has shaped our view of them. We have seen the Queen a million times, but most of us would find it easier to describe the appearance of Elizabeth I, based as it is on a few decisive archetypes.

The state portrait, like so much royal ceremonial, has lost its meaning in modern times, and it is to be found only in the most traditional of institutions. Not only has the quality of portrait painting declined, but few recent artists have given any thought to the deeper problems of royal iconography. The present queen has sat to more artists than any of her predecessors, but her connection with them is very tenuous. Earlier monarchs had a relationship with their painters, and a mutual understanding of one another's function. Today, portraits of the Queen are commissioned by outside bodies, and she is posed on the model stand for as long as it takes the artist to record her likeness. This is not the atmosphere in which symbolic portraiture can flourish, and the results are predictably superficial.

The Edwardian age saw the demise of formal portraiture as a creative art form. Edward VII himself seems to have had a limited interest in the arts, and he sat to some of the duller artists of the period. He might have been painted by J. S. Sargent, an artist of great style and panache, but Sargent was only employed as an afterthought to record the king on his deathbed (*Plate 141*). The best picture of Edward as king is by A. S. Cope, a well-designed and strongly painted work that catches some of the subject's vitality and ebullience in the sharp turn of the head, and the fluttering garter robes (*Plates 138 and 139*). Cope continued in royal service, but his later portraits of George V are empty parade pieces (*Plate 145*), and he never repeated his success.

Few painters have managed to resist the slide towards mediocrity. In 1913, John Lavery painted what must rank as the last distinguished royal group (*Plate 144*). The setting is the White Drawing Room in Buckingham Palace, and a cool and silvery light filters through the windows of this imposing room. The figures are a little puppet-like, but we have here a modern interpretation of the grand state machine, and it is sufficiently well painted to carry conviction. According to the artist, George V was so pleased with the portrait that he painted a small part of the garter ribbon. Charles Sims was less fortunate in this respect. His official portrait of George V (1924) placed too much emphasis on the sitter's elegant legs and out-turned feet, rather in the spirit of Lely. The king thought that he looked too much like a ballet dancer, and the offending canvas was destroyed. The most interesting painted images of George V are two portraits by Sickert (*Plate 147*), both based on press photographs. Sickert liked the freedom which this method of work gave him, without the need for commissions or sittings. He exploited the medium of photography to create highly original works of art.

Sickert was one of the few artists to paint Edward VIII during his brief reign, again after a photograph (*Plate 155*). The troubled and uncertain expression of the sitter is oddly evocative, and it contrasts with the broad, vigorous touches of the painting. Although derivative as a likeness, the picture has infinitely more force than conventional studies from the life.

The official coronation portraits of George VI and Queen Elizabeth the Queen Mother were painted by Sir Gerald Kelly (*Plate 156*). He records how self-conscious and uncomfortable the king felt in his coronation costume, which was 'almost a stage garment. . . . I had to try and solve the problem of persuading this modest man to strike some decorative pose, because I had got it firmly into my head that a State Portrait should be romantically decorative.' The grand background was painted from the model of a marble hall designed for the artist by Sir Edwin Lutyens in the style of his palace at Delhi—one of the last great imperial monuments. Kelly took immense pains to work out the perspective and lighting of the figure and background, and the picture was elaborated with the utmost precision. It perhaps required this conscious effort for a modern artist to overcome the problems of designing on a grandiose scale, and the result is impressive, if a little chilly.

The most successful portrait of the present queen is the one by Annigoni, painted for the Fishmongers' Company (*Plates 1 and 167*). The key to success here is the artist's skill in investing a traditional image of majesty with genuine glamour and romance. The dignity of the radiant young queen, posed in a dark garter mantle against a winter landscape, is very touching. One is reminded of certain Renaissance portraits where the contrast between figure and setting is similarly dramatic. Annigoni is a master of the striking effect, and a realist painter with a virtuoso technique. Most of his rivals do not even get marks for likeness, and recent portraits of the Queen are, by and large, disappointing.

If painted portraits of the royal family have lost their power to impress us, it cannot be said that photography offers an altogether adequate substitute. It is no easier with the camera than the brush to convey those qualities inseparable from the idea of monarchy. Most photographers rely on our conditioned response to a few conventional props, without giving them meaning or life.

A distinction must be drawn between the studio and the press photograph. Those in the first category are usually commissioned, often in connection with a royal occasion, and they are issued with the approval of the Palace, under certain clearly defined conditions. The scale of fees is fixed in advance, and all members of the press have access to the prints at the same time, and on the same terms. The royal family have always been keenly alive to the importance of photography, and they have shown a refreshing willingness to experiment and to change with the times.

Official photographs of the royal family during the reigns of Edward VII and George V tended to be taken by the large commercial studios like W. & D. Downey, Bassano and Vandyk. Stiffly posed in robes of state, with ermine trains carefully arranged on the steps of a dais, they often look like waxworks, an illusion heightened in the painted versions, produced by the studio artists for exhibition purposes. Even the group pictures are characterized by a frozen immobility (*Plate 152*). Cecil Beaton remarked that the royal family have been photographed so often in formal attitudes 'that it is almost impossible to break down the results of their training to stand in line' (*Photobiography*, 1951).

Press photographs, by contrast with studio productions, show the king and queen as figures of the everyday world, and they are often more revealing of likeness and character. Royalty conducted themselves with more formality in the early years of the century, and press photographers showed greater discretion. But the techniques of the action shot and the close-up were developed early on, and there are some delightfully unguarded studies of the royal family. The chief problem with press photographs is repetition. If one has seen the king or queen shaking hands once, one has seen it ten thousand times, and the same goes for visiting factories, opening buildings and attending functions. Images quickly lose their impact in this world of official duties and ceremonies—the same set smiles and attitudes, the slightly constrained atmosphere of deference and decorum. Everybody is on their best behaviour and anxious to please.

The studio photographs of George VI and Queen Elizabeth the Queen Mother offer an interesting guide to changing styles and fashions. George VI had a tendency to look the same, whoever was photographing him, but the Queen Mother is a wonderfully responsive and photogenic subject, who radiates charm and vitality. The photographs taken at the time of their wedding in 1923 are formal and impersonal. In the 1930s, they sat to fashionable society photographers like Dorothy Wilding and Bertram Park, purveyors of a soft-focus, sentimental style. James and Lisa Sheridan made their reputation with a long series of informal and naturalistic studies of the royal family out of doors. In 1939, Cecil Beaton was invited to photograph the Queen Mother, and so began a long and distinguished career as a court photographer.

Cecil Beaton is a conjuror with images who interprets his sitters in terms of brilliant scenic effects. He can change from austere realism to fashionable chic or surrealist fantasy as easily as he substitutes sets. His inventiveness is linked to an acute awareness of the social and intellectual tone of the people he photographs. Posing the Queen Mother in billowing crinoline dresses of silver and gold, complete with tiara and jewellery, against soft aureoles of light, he established a romantic vision of her as the beautiful and graceful queen of a fairy-tale kingdom. The backgrounds are grandiose: echoing palatial rooms; or painted sets from eighteenth-century masterpieces, Panini's *Ruined Archway* and Fragonard's *Swing* (*Plate 157*), the central incidents of which have been replaced by dazzling back projections of light; or out-of-door settings, where, with parasol and hat, she poses under a giant stone vase, or by the baroque statuary of a summer house. No member of the royal family can have been photographed in quite such impressive and seductive surroundings. 'For how could I fail to make entrancing pictures?' writes Beaton, 'The bright and sympathetically wistful eyes regarded me with an uncompromising kindliness. With the minimum of effort the mouth forms a smile which is as fresh as a dewdrop and no creases are ever formed at its sides; the arms and wrists are white and rounded as those of an early Victorian marble statue; the hands are country hands . . . the appearance combines that of a child and a great lady.'

Cecil Beaton is far and away the most successful royal photographer of modern times. His photographs are royal images in the true sense, and, however much they may rely on artifice and pastiche, they are admirably composed and very dramatic in effect. The coronation photograph of the present queen is an essay in state portraiture of the most formal kind (*Plate 168*), and it can challenge comparison with Hayter's coronation picture of Queen Victoria (*Plate 123*). Equally monumental is the photograph of the Queen in garter robes and hat, a pyramid shape silhouetted against a painted back-drop of Windsor Castle. Beaton is eminently versatile, and his informal photographs of the royal family are brilliant essays in naturalistic portraiture, like the groups of the present queen with her children (*Plate 172*).

The only photographer who has come close to Beaton's achievement is Baron. He has a strong feeling for mood and setting, and his formal photographs are more static and severe than Beaton's, but scarcely less impressive. He describes his career as a royal photographer in his book of reminiscences: 'By 1950 my camera and I had been witnesses to many if not most of the important celebrations of the Royal Family. We were at the wedding of Princess Elizabeth and Prince Philip; at the christening, first of Prince Charles and then of Princess Anne; at the twenty-fifth wedding anniversary of King George VI and Queen Elizabeth, and at the twentieth birthday of Princess Margaret.' More recently photographers of the royal family include Lord Snowdon, Patrick Lichfield, who took the silver wedding group (*Plate 166*), and Norman Parkinson, whose *Vogue* eye view of Princess Anne established a new royal look (*Plate 176*).

The latest development in royal iconography is the royal film, pioneered by Richard Cawston in his famous documentary of 1969, from which *Plate 173* is a still. The illusion of being allowed behind the façade of monarchy, to see the royal family as ordinary individuals enjoying their own lives, is cunningly presented. The barrier of grandeur and reserve appears to have fallen away as part of a process of drawing the monarchy closer to the people. Like Queen

Victoria's enthusiastic response to photography, the present royal family has taken advantage of a modern medium to present a view of themselves that is tactfully edited. No doubt the film does mark a watershed in the visual treatment of royalty, going further than ever before in its informal view of royal life. But it is careful to preserve the mystique of monarchy, and one can question how far it is possible or desirable to go in exposing the private lives of its members.

List of plates

The plates

1. HER MAJESTY QUEEN ELIZABETH II. *Painting by Pietro Annigoni, 1955 (detail of Plate 167)*

2. THE CORONATION, OR KING EDWARD'S CHAIR, IN WESTMINSTER ABBEY, LONDON. *It encloses the Stone of Scone and has been used at every coronation since that of Edward II in 1308.*

3. WILLIAM I. *Detail from the Bayeux Tapestry*

4. WILLIAM I.
Seal by an Unknown Artist

5. WILLIAM I. *Coin by Ordric of Gloucester*

6. WILLIAM II. *Coin by Lifsun of Maldon*

7. HENRY I.
Seal by an Unknown Artist

8. HENRY I. *Coin by Wulfgar of London*

9. STEPHEN. *Coin by William of Carlisle (enlarged)*

10. HENRY II. *Coin by Isaac of York (enlarged)*

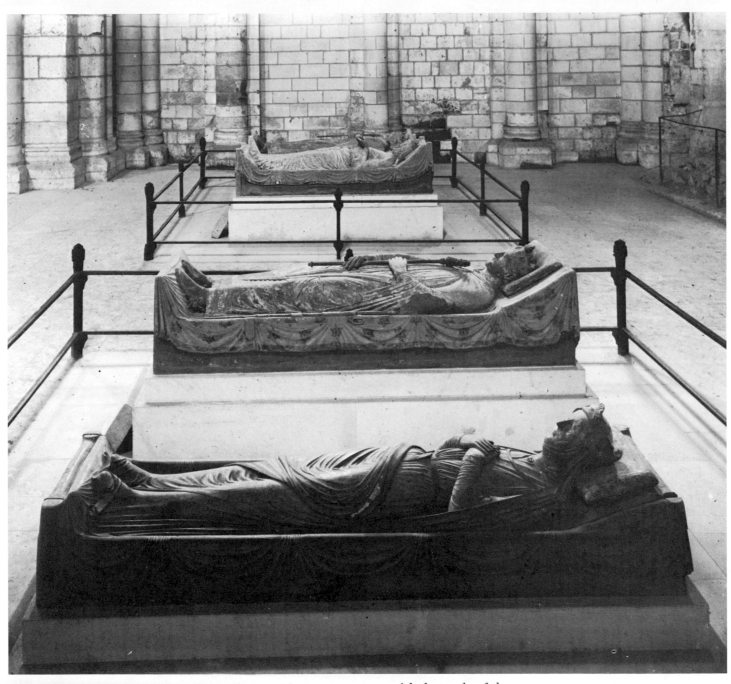

11. INTERIOR OF FONTEVRAULT ABBEY, MAINE-ET-LOIRE, *with the tombs of the early Plantagenets*

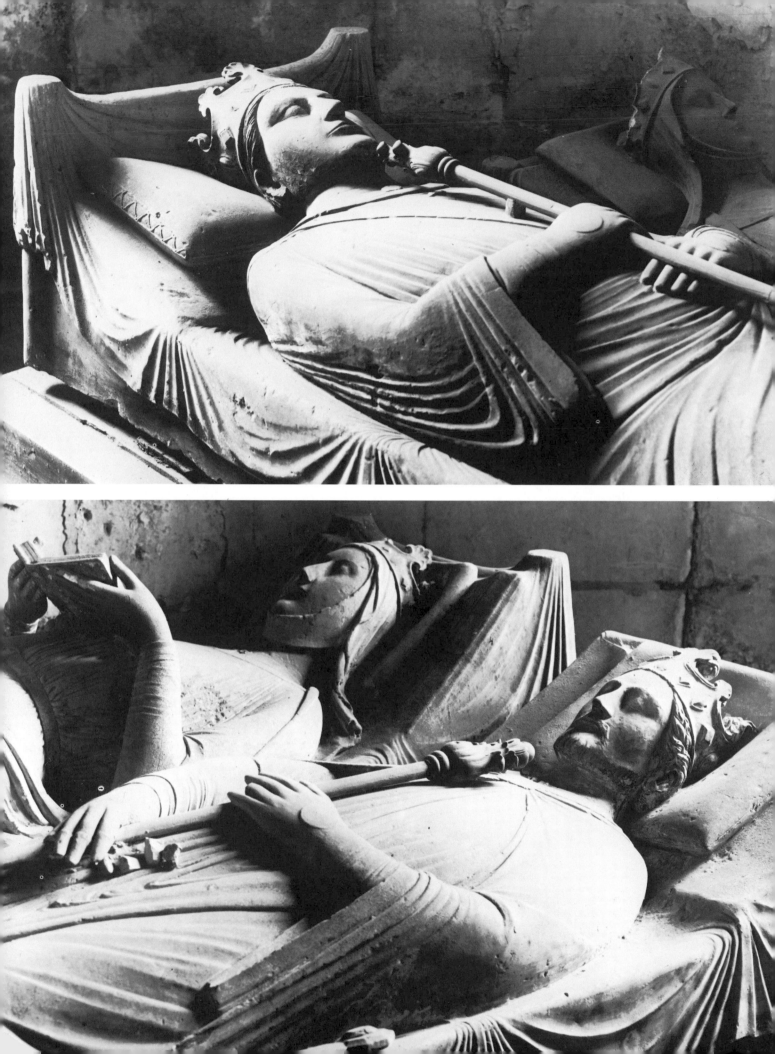

14. RICHARD I. *Effigy in Fontevrault Abbey by an Unknown Artist*

12. (*above*) HENRY II. *Detail of effigy in Fontevrault Abbey by an Unknown Artist*

13. (*below*) RICHARD I AND ELEANOR OF AQUITAINE. *Detail of effigies in Fontevrault Abbey*

15. JOHN. *Detail of effigy in Worcester Cathedral by an Unknown Artist, about 1225–30*

16. HENRY III. *Effigy in Westminster Abbey by William Torel, about 1291*

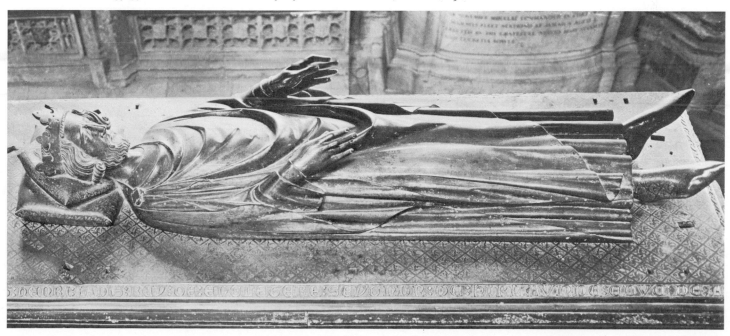

17. ELEANOR OF CASTILE. *Detail of effigy in Westminster Abbey by William Torel, about 1291*

18. HENRY III. *Detail of Plate 16*

19. EDWARD II'S TOMB. *In Gloucester Cathedral, about 1330*

22. (*opposite*) EDWARD II. *Effigy in Gloucester Cathedral by an Unknown Artist, about 1330*

21. EDWARD I. *Coin by an Unknown Artist, about 1279*

20. EDWARD I. *Seal by an Unknown Artist*

23. EDWARD III. *Detail of tomb effigy in Westminster Abbey by an Unknown Artist, about 1377–80*

24. EDWARD III. *Detail of funeral effigy in Westminster Abbey attributed to Stephen Hadley, 1377*

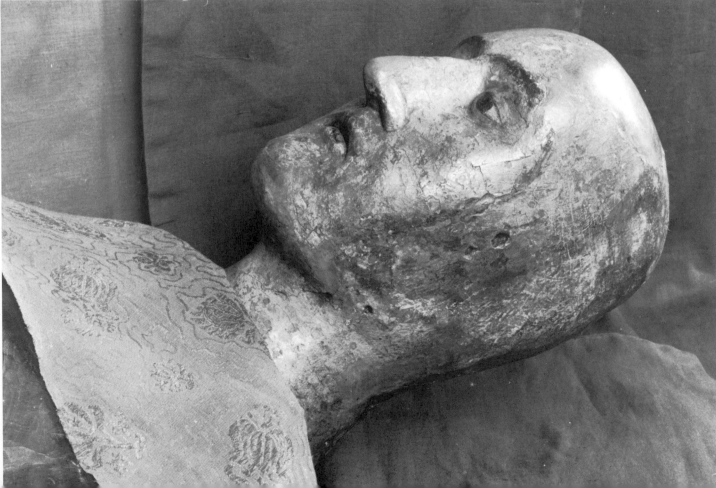

25. RICHARD II. *Infra-red photograph, detail of Plate 26*

26. RICHARD II. *Painting in Westminster Abbey by an Unknown Artist*

27. RICHARD II. *Painting by an Unknown Artist (detail of the 'Wilton Diptych')*

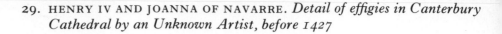

29. HENRY IV AND JOANNA OF NAVARRE. *Detail of effigies in Canterbury Cathedral by an Unknown Artist, before 1427*

28. HENRY V. *Miniature from 'De Regimine Principum' by an Unknown Artist*

30. EDWARD IV IN COUNCIL. *Miniature by an Unknown Artist, about 1470–1*

31. HENRY VI. *Painting by an Unknown Artist*

32. EDWARD IV. *Painting by an Unknown Artist, about 1472*

33. EDWARD V WHEN PRINCE OF WALES. *Stained glass by an Unknown Artist, about 1482*

34. RICHARD III. *Painting by an Unknown Artist*

35. HENRY VII. *Painting by Michael Sittow, 1505*

36. HENRY VII. *Bust attributed to Pietro Torrigiano*

37. HENRY VII. *Detail of effigy in Westminster Abbey by Pietro Torrigiano, 1519–20*

313

38. HENRY VIII. *Painting attributed to Joos van Cleve, about 1535*

39. HENRY VIII. *Painting by Hans Holbein, 1536*

40. HENRY VIII. *Painting by an*
Unknown Artist after Hans Holbein

41. HENRY VII, ELIZABETH OF YORK,
HENRY VIII AND JANE SEYMOUR.
Painting by Remigius van Leemput
after Hans Holbein

42. HENRY VIII. *Detail of cartoon by Hans Holbein, about 1536*

43. CATHERINE OF ARAGON. *Painting by an Unknown Artist*

44. ANNE BOLEYN. *Painting by an Unknown Artist*

46. CATHERINE PARR. *Painting by an Unknown Artist*

No authentic portrait of CATHERINE HOWARD, Henry VIII's fifth wife, is known

45. ANNE OF CLEVES. *Painting by Hans Holbein, 1539*

47. JANE SEYMOUR. *Detail of painting by Hans Holbein, about 1536*

48. THE FAMILY OF HENRY VIII. *Painting attributed to Lucas de Heere, about 1570*

49. EDWARD VI AND THE POPE. *Painting by an Unknown Artist, about 1548*

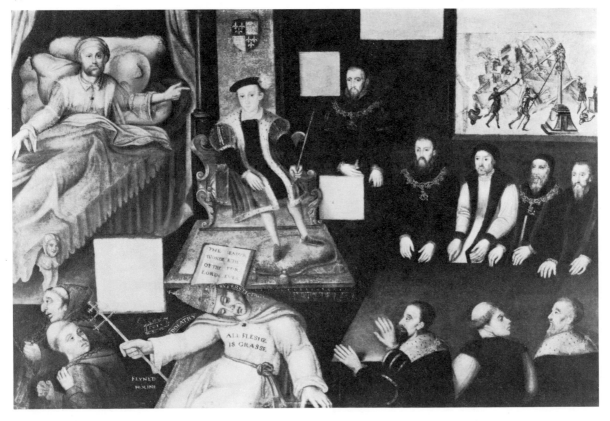

50. ELIZABETH I
SITTING IN
JUDGEMENT OF
THE POPE.
*Engraving by
Pieter van der
Heyden, 1584–5*

51. ELIZABETH I AND
THE THREE
GODDESSES.
*Painting
attributed to Hans
Eworth, 1569*

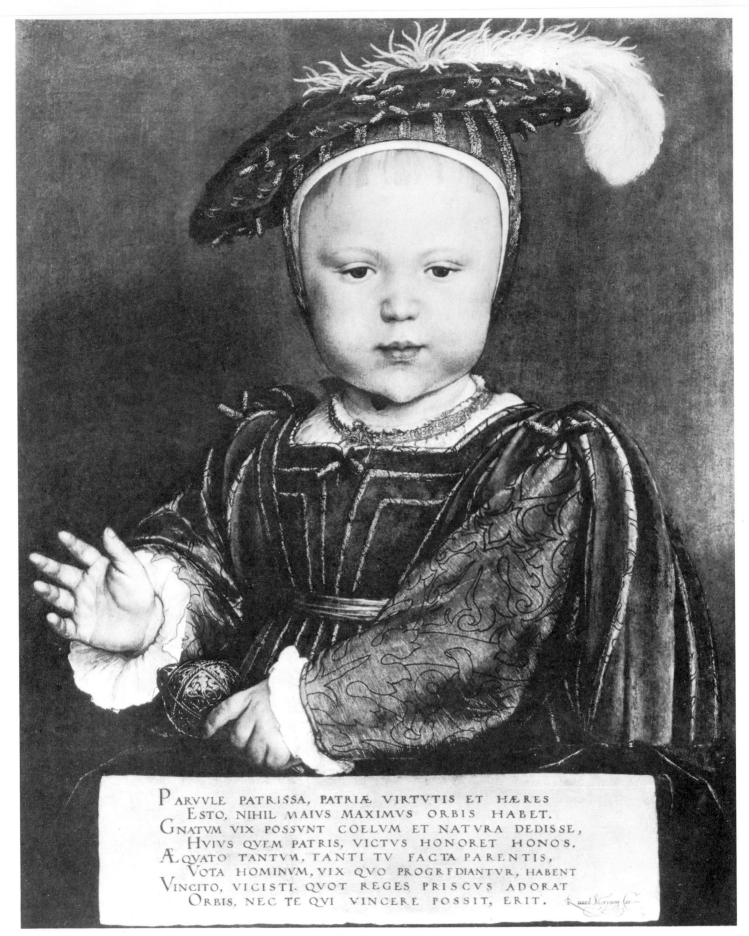

PARVVLE PATRISSA, PATRIÆ VIRTVTIS ET HÆRES
ESTO, NIHIL MAIVS MAXIMVS ORBIS HABET.
GNATVM VIX POSSVNT COELVM ET NATVRA DEDISSE,
HVIVS QVEM PATRIS, VICTVS HONORET HONOS.
ÆQVATO TANTVM, TANTI TV FACTA PARENTIS,
VOTA HOMINVM, VIX QVO PROGREDIANTVR, HABENT
VINCITO, VICISTI. QVOT REGES PRISCVS ADORAT
ORBIS, NEC TE QVI VINCERE POSSIT, ERIT. *Ruard Morsun Car-*

52. EDWARD VI WHEN PRINCE EDWARD. *Painting by Hans Holbein, 1539*

53. EDWARD VI. *Painting attributed to William Scrots, about 1550*

54 & 55. MARY I. *Painting by Anthonis Mor, 1554*

NON SINE SOLE
IRIS.

57. ELIZABETH I. *Painting by an Unknown Artist* (*The 'Rainbow portrait'*), *about 1600*

56. (*opposite*) ELIZABETH I WHEN PRINCESS ELIZABETH. *Painting by an Unknown Artist, about 1546*

58 & 59. ELIZABETH I. *Painting attributed to George Gower, about 1588*

60. ELIZABETH I. *Miniature by Nicholas Hilliard, 1572*

61. ELIZABETH I. *Miniature*
by Isaac Oliver, about 1590

62. ELIZABETH I. *Miniature by Nicholas*
Hilliard, about 1590

63. ELIZABETH I. *Engraving by William Rogers, about 1590*

64. JAMES I. *Painting by John de Critz, about 1606*

65. (*below left*) JAMES I. *Miniature by Nicholas Hilliard, about 1603–8*

66. (*below centre*) JAMES I. *Miniature by John Hoskins, after Paul Van Somer*

67. (*below right*) ANNE OF DENMARK. *Miniature by Isaac Oliver*

Who viewes not on this reverend aspect
Wisdome and Maiesty theire rayes reflect?
Under whome Faiths defence hath florisht ever
Under whome Peace and vertue aye persever
Whose cost and care in heathen Lands doe place
Gods word; whose workes foule heresie deface
Each where admir'd each where renown'd abroad
Deere to his Subiects, deerest to his God:
Long live; and now in heaven thy soule doth raigne
May stil thy name, thy love, on earth remaine.

And thou great Prince) enricht with prudent heart,
So form'd by nature soe well fram'd by art
In truths right way as thou didst heare goe on
That thou now liust in heauen a Solomon
Passe Davids valour, and thy Sires loud fame,
And that though dead the world may found thy name

Anno Doni
1621.

With: Passæus figu: et sculpsit.

Georg: Fearebeard excuta

68. JAMES I AND HENRY, PRINCE OF WALES. *Engraving by William van de Passe, 1621*

69. HENRY FREDERICK, PRINCE OF WALES, AND HIS FRIEND, JOHN, LORD HARRINGTON OF EXTON, IN THE HUNTING FIELD. *Painting attributed to Robert Peake the Elder, 1603*

The high
and mighty PRINCE
CHARLES, PRINCE of
Great Brittayn. and Ireland.
Duke of Yorke and Albany.
Marquis of Ormont: &c.
And Knight of the most
noble order of the
Garter.

ICH DIEN

Renold
Elstrack sculp.

Are to be sould at the whit horse, in Popes:
head Alley, by Iohn Sudbury, and George Humble

From Two great kingdomes match'd in Royall blood, May thy faire spring, in Sommers glory bud, Synce in thy brest the hope of Brittayns Name
the Sacred Stemmes of Kingly Auncestry, Euen to the height of Rule, and Dignity, lyes hid As in a Cabynet of Fame ✶

70. CHARLES I WHEN PRINCE OF WALES. *Engraving by Renold Elstrack, about 1614–15*

71. CHARLES I. *Detail of Plate 72*

72. CHARLES I AND HENRIETTA
MARIA DEPARTING FOR THE
CHASE. *Painting by Daniel
Mytens, about 1630–2*

73. CHARLES I. *Painting by Gerard Honthorst, about 1628*

74. THE FIVE ELDEST CHILDREN OF CHARLES I. *Painting by Sir Anthony van Dyck, 1637*

75. CHARLES I ON HORSEBACK WITH MONSEIGNEUR
DE SAINT ANTOINE IN ATTENDANCE. *Painting by
Sir Anthony van Dyck, 1633*

76 & 79. HENRIETTA MARIA. *Painting by
Sir Anthony van Dyck, 1632*

77. HENRIETTA MARIA. *Detail of Plate 72*

78. HENRIETTA MARIA. *Miniature by John Hoskins*

80. CHARLES I. *Bust by François Dusart, 1636*

81. CHARLES I. *Detail of statue by Hubert Le Sueur, 1633*

82 & 83. CHARLES I IN THREE POSITIONS. *Painting by Sir Anthony van Dyck, about 1635*

84. CHARLES I WITH HIS SON, JAMES, DUKE OF YORK. *Painting by Sir Peter Lely, 1647*

85. CHARLES I AT HIS TRIAL. *Painting by Edward Bower, 1648*

86. THE EXECUTION OF
CHARLES I. *Engraving
by an Unknown
Artist, 1649*

87. CHARLES I. *Engraving
by William Marshall,
about 1648*

88. THE GREAT FEAST THE ESTATES OF HOLLAND MADE TO THE KING AND TO THE ROYAL FAMILY. *Engraving by Pierre Philippe after Jacob Toorenvliet*

89. CHARLES II AND HIS SISTER, MARY, PRINCESS OF ORANGE, AT A BALL AT THE HAGUE. *Detail of painting by Hieronymus Janssens, 1660*

92. CHARLES II. *Bust by Honoré Pelle, 1684*

90. CHARLES II. *Miniature by Samuel Cooper, 1665*

91. CATHERINE OF BRAGANZA.
Miniature by Samuel Cooper

93. CHARLES II. *Painting attributed to Hendrik Dankerts, after 1670*

94. CHARLES II.
*Painting by
Sir Peter
Lely, about
1675*

95. JAMES II WHEN DUKE OF YORK. *Miniature by Samuel Cooper, 1670–2*

96. JAMES II. *Painting by Nicholas de Largillière, about 1686*

97. JAMES II.
*Painting by
Sir Godfrey
Kneller,
1684*

98. WILLIAM III. *Painting by Godfried Schalcken, about 1692*

100. WILLIAM III. *Detail of wax effigy, without wig, in Westminster Abbey attributed to Mrs Goldsmith*

99. WILLIAM III. *Bust by Jan Blommendael, 1699*

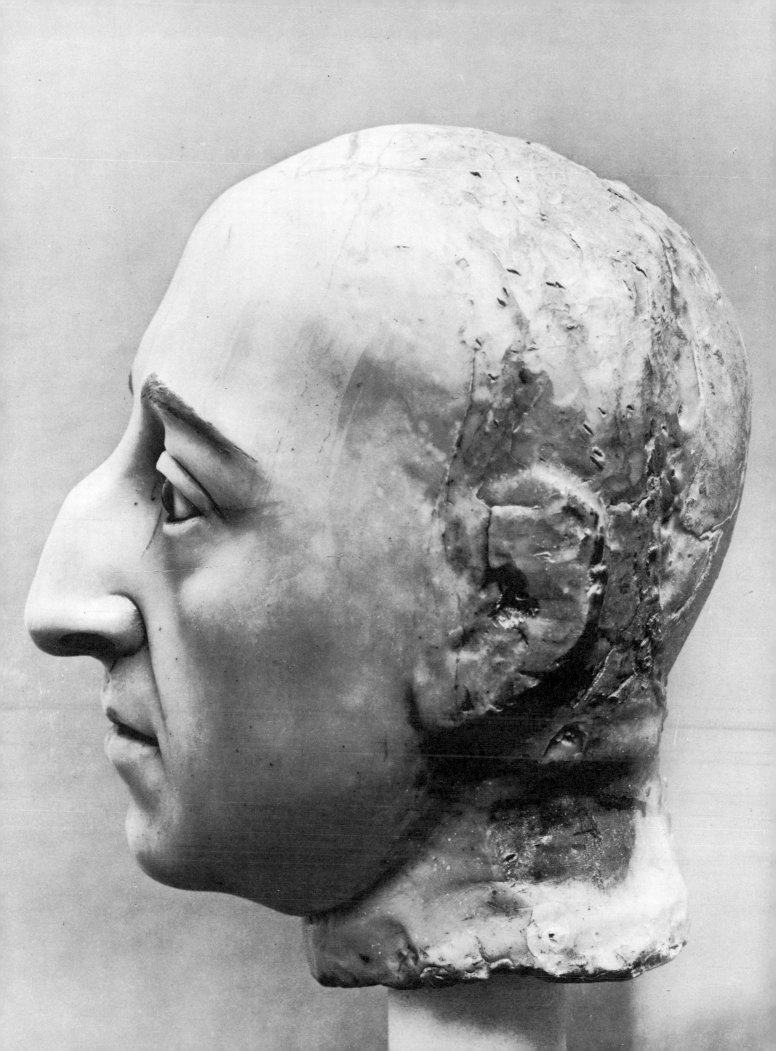

101. MARY II. *Effigy in Westminster Abbey attributed to Mrs Goldsmith*

102. QUEEN
ANNE.
*Painting by
Edmund
Lilly, 1703*

103. GEORGE I. *Painting by Sir James Thornhill, 1714–15*

104. GEORGE I. *Bust by Michael Rysbrack*

105. FREDERICK, PRINCE OF WALES, AND HIS
SISTERS. *Painting by Philip Mercier, 1733*

106. GEORGE II. *Painting by John Shackleton, 1758*

108. GEORGE II. *Bust by Louis François Roubiliac*

107. GEORGE II. *Caricature by George, 1st Marquess Townshend*

109. GEORGE III. *Painting by Allan Ramsay, 1760*

110. GEORGE III. *Painting by Allan Ramsay, 1760*

111. GEORGE III. *Bust by Agostino Carlini, 1773*

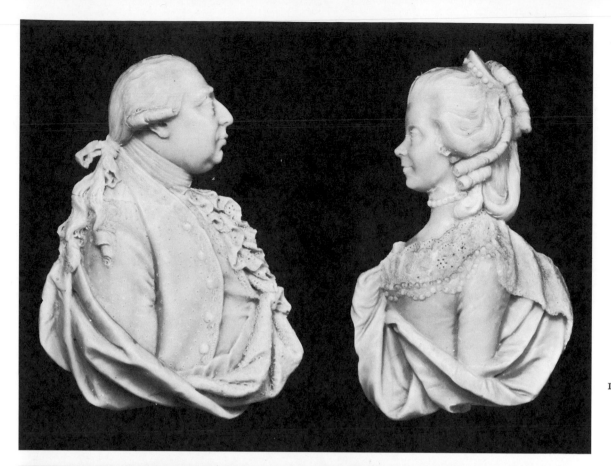

112. GEORGE III AND QUEEN CHARLOTTE. *Medallions by Samuel Percy*

113. QUEEN CHARLOTTE WITH HER TWO ELDEST SONS. *Painting by Johann Zoffany, about 1765*

A VOLUPTUARY under the horrors of Digestion.

114. A VOLUPTUARY UNDER THE HORRORS OF DIGESTION (GEORGE IV WHEN PRINCE OF WALES).
    Caricature by James Gillray, 1792

GEORGE. P.
TO FRANCIS EARL OF MOIRA.

115. GEORGE IV
WHEN
PRINCE OF
WALES.
*Painting by
Sir Joshua
Reynolds,
1787*

116. GEORGE IV.
*Painting by
Sir Thomas
Lawrence,
1821*

117. CAROLINE OF BRUNSWICK. *Bust by Anne Seymour Damer, 1814*

118. GEORGE IV WHEN PRINCE OF WALES. *Painting by Sir Thomas Lawrence, about 1814*

119. WILLIAM IV. *Bust by Sir Francis Chantrey, 1837*

120. WILLIAM IV WHEN DUKE OF CLARENCE. *Study by Sir Thomas
Lawrence, about 1827*

121. WILLIAM IV. *Painting by Sir David Wilkie, 1833*

123. THE CORONATION OF
VICTORIA. *Detail of
engraving by H. T.
Ryall after Sir George
Hayter*

122. ADELAIDE. *Painting by
Sir Martin Archer Shee,
about 1837*

124. WINDSOR CASTLE IN MODERN TIMES. *Painting by Sir Edwin Landseer, about 1842*

125. VICTORIA AND ALBERT AS CATHERINE OF BRAGANZA
AND CHARLES II. *Painting by F. X. Winterhalter, 1851*

126. VICTORIA AND ALBERT DRESSED AS
ANGLO-SAXONS. *Statue by William
Theed, about 1868*

127. VICTORIA AND ALBERT AS QUEEN PHILIPPA AND EDWARD III. *Painting by Sir Edwin Landseer, 1842*

128. VICTORIA. *Painting by
F. X. Winterhalter, 1843*

129. VICTORIA WITH THE
PRINCESS ROYAL.
*Calotype attributed to
Henry Collen, 1844–5*

130. 'THE FIRST OF MAY, 1851.' *Painting by F. X. Winterhalter, 1851*

131. VICTORIA AND HER FAMILY. *Calotype by Roger Fenton, 1854*

132. VICTORIA WITH THE PRINCE
AND PRINCESS OF WALES.
*Photograph by J. P. Mayall,
1863*

133. EDWARD VII WHEN PRINCE OF
WALES WITH HIS WIFE AND
CHILDREN. *Painting by
Heinrich von Angeli, about 1876*

A VISION.

V——."WHY DO YOU FROWN—WHAT HAVE I DONE?"   E——."LET GRIEF PREVAIL O'ER DUTY!"

134. A VISION. *Woodcut by an Unknown Artist, 1868*

135. VICTORIA WITH AN INDIAN ATTENDANT AT FROGMORE. *Photograph by Hills & Saunders*

136. THE ROYAL FAMILY AT THE TIME OF THE JUBILEE. *Painting by Laurits Tuxen, 1887*

1. Queen Victoria, 2. The Prince of Wales, 3. The Princess of Wales, 4. Prince Albert Victor, 5. Prince George of Wales, 6. Princess Louise of Wales, 7. Princess Victoria of Wales, 8. Princess Maud of Wales, 9. Crown Princess of Germany, 10. Crown Prince of Germany, 11. Prince William of Prussia, 12. Princess William of Prussia, 13. Prince Frederick William of Prussia, 14. The Hereditary Princess of Saxe-Meiningen, 15. The Hereditary Prince of Saxe-Meiningen, 16. Princess Theodore of Saxe-Meiningen, 17. Prince Henry of Prussia, 18. Princess Irene of Hesse, 19. Princess Victoria of Prussia, 20. Princess Sophie of Prussia, 21. Princess Margaret of Prussia, 22. The Grand Duke of Hesse, 23. Princess Louis of Battenberg, 24. Prince Louis of Battenberg, 25. Princess Alice of Battenberg, 26. The Grand Duchess Elizabeth of Russia, 27. The Grand Duke Serge of Russia, 28. The Hereditary Grand Duke of Hesse, 29. Princess Alix of Hesse, 30. The Duke of Edinburgh, 31. The Duchess of Edinburgh, 32. Prince Alfred of Edinburgh, 33. Princess Marie of Edinburgh, 34. Princess Victoria Melita of Edinburgh, 35. Princess Alexandra of Edinburgh, 36. Princess Beatrice of Edinburgh, 37. Princess Christian of Schleswig-Holstein, Princess Helena of Great Britain and Ireland, 38. Prince Christian of Schleswig-Holstein, 39. Prince Christian Victor of Schleswig-Holstein, 40. Prince Albert of Schleswig-Holstein, 41. Princess Victoria of Schleswig-Holstein, 42. Princess Louise of Schleswig-Holstein, 43. Princess Louise, Marchioness of Lorne, 44. The Marquis of Lorne, 45. The Duke of Connaught, 46. The Duchess of Connaught, 47. Princess Margaret of Connaught, 48. Prince Arthur of Connaught, 49. Princess Victoria Beatrice Patricia of Connaught, 50. The Duchess of Albany, 51. Princess Alice of Albany, 52. Prince Charles Edward, Duke of Albany, 53. Princess Beatrice, Princess Henry of Battenberg, 54. Prince Henry of Battenberg, 55. Prince Alexander Albert of Battenberg.

137. THE FOUR GENERATIONS. *Photograph by W. & D. Downey, 1894*

138 & 139. EDWARD VII. *Painting by Sir Arthur S. Cope, 1907*

140. THE THREE GENERATIONS.
Press photograph, 1909

141. EDWARD VII ON HIS
DEATHBED. *Sketch by John
Singer Sargent, 1910*

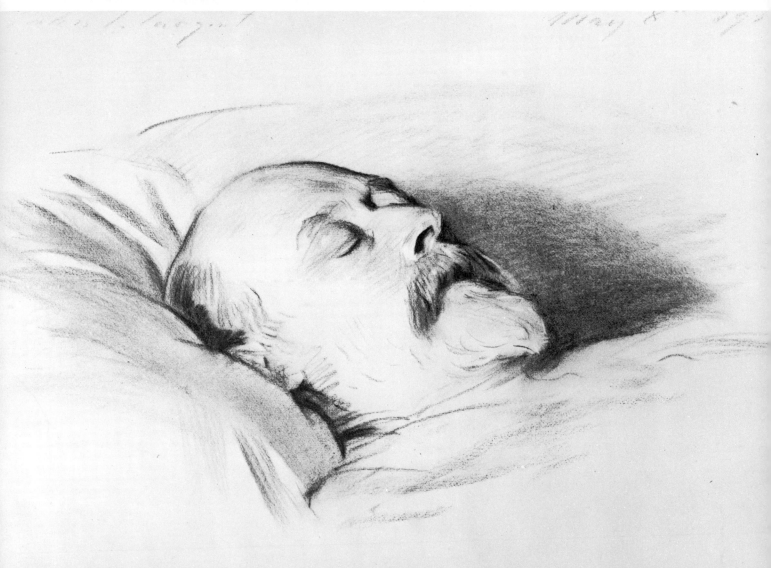

142. QUEEN MARY AND QUEEN ALEXANDRA. *Photograph by Mrs Albert Broom, 1915*

143. THE DELHI DURBAR. *Press photograph, 1911*

144. THE ROYAL FAMILY AT BUCKINGHAM PALACE. *Painting by Sir John Lavery, 1913*

145. GEORGE V. *Painting
by Sir Arthur S. Cope, 1913*

146. GEORGE V. *Press photograph, 1920*

147. A CONVERSATION
PIECE AT AINTREE.
*Painting by
W. R. Sickert, about
1927–30*

148. GEORGE V *with his trainer, Major Featherstonaugh,
at Aintree. Press photograph, 1927*

149. GEORGE V. *Press photograph*

150. QUEEN ELIZABETH THE QUEEN
MOTHER WHEN LADY
ELIZABETH BOWES-LYON.
Photograph by Vandyk, 1922

151. QUEEN ELIZABETH THE QUEEN MOTHER
WHEN DUCHESS OF YORK. *Painting by
Philip de Laszlo, 1925*

152. THE ROYAL
FAMILY.
*Photograph by
Bassano, 1923*

153. GEORGE VI AND QUEEN
ELIZABETH THE QUEEN
MOTHER WHEN DUKE AND
DUCHESS OF YORK. *Press
photograph, 1929*

154. EDWARD VIII WHEN PRINCE OF WALES AT MINERS' COTTAGES IN NORTHUMBERLAND. *Press photograph, 1929*

155. EDWARD VIII. *Painting by
W. R. Sickert, 1936*

156. GEORGE VI. *Painting by Sir Gerald Kelly, 1938–45*

157. QUEEN ELIZABETH THE QUEEN MOTHER. *Photograph by Cecil Beaton, 1940*

158. GEORGE VI AND QUEEN ELIZABETH THE QUEEN MOTHER WITH PRINCESS ELIZABETH AND PRINCESS MARGARET. *Press photograph, 1934*

159. QUEEN MARY WITH HER MAJESTY THE QUEEN WHEN PRINCESS ELIZABETH. *Press photograph, 1938*

160. HARVEST AT SANDRINGHAM. *Press photograph, 1943*

161. QUEEN ELIZABETH THE QUEEN MOTHER INSPECTING THE CITIZENS' ADVICE BUREAU. *Press photograph, 1942*

162. GEORGE VI WITH HER
MAJESTY THE QUEEN
WHEN PRINCESS
ELIZABETH. *Press
photograph, 1945*

163. PRINCESS MARGARET AT A FASHION SHOW. *Press photograph, 1951*

164. HER MAJESTY THE QUEEN WHEN PRINCESS ELIZABETH, AND PRINCE PHILIP. *Press photograph, 1947*

165. THE CHRISTENING OF PRINCE MICHAEL OF KENT. *Press photograph, 1942*

1. Princess Marie Louise, 2. Prince Bernhard of the Netherlands, 3. King George VI, 4. The Duke of Kent, 5. King Haakon of Norway, 6. King George of the Hellenes, 7. Crown Prince Olaf of Norway, 8. Princess Elizabeth, 9. Lady Patricia Ramsay, 10. Queen Elizabeth, 11. Prince Edward of Kent, 12. Queen Mary, 13. Princess Alexandra, 14. The Duchess of Kent with the infant prince, 15. The Dowager Marchioness of Milford Haven, 16. Crown Princess Marthe of Norway, 17. Princess Margaret, 18. Princess Helena Victoria.

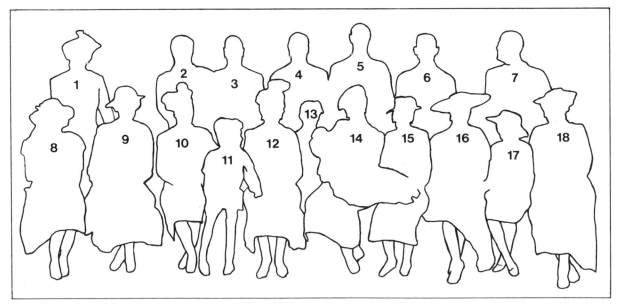

166. SILVER WEDDING GROUP. *Photograph by Patrick Lichfield, 1972*

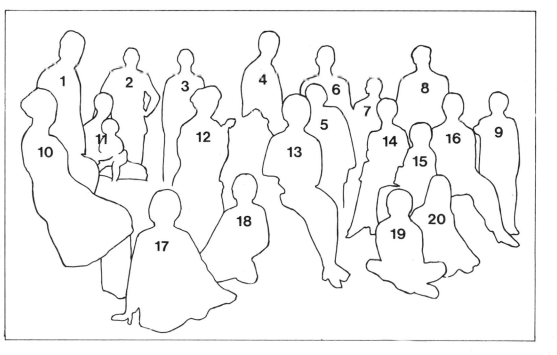

1. Lord Snowdon, 2. The Duke of Kent, 3. Prince Michael of Kent, 4. The Duke of Edinburgh, 5. Lord St Andrews, 6. The Prince of Wales, 7. Prince Andrew, 8. Mr Angus Ogilvy, 9. James Ogilvy, 10. Princess Margaret, 11. The Duchess of Kent (holding Lord Nicholas Windsor), 12. Queen Elizabeth the Queen Mother, 13. Queen Elizabeth II, 14. Princess Anne, 15. Marina Ogilvy, 16. Princess Alexandra, 17. Lady Sarah Armstrong-Jones, 18. Lord Linley, 19. Prince Edward, 20. Lady Helen Windsor.

167. HER MAJESTY QUEEN ELIZABETH II. *Painting by Pietro Annigoni, 1955*

168. HER MAJESTY QUEEN ELIZABETH II. *Photograph by Cecil Beaton, 1953*

169. HER MAJESTY QUEEN
ELIZABETH II. *Press
photograph, 1953*

171. (*opposite*) HER MAJESTY
THE QUEEN WHEN
PRINCESS ELIZABETH.
Press photograph, 1949

170. HER MAJESTY QUEEN ELIZABETH II
TALKING TO MRS WINIFRED GASKIN.
Press photograph, 1966

172 HER MAJESTY QUEEN ELIZABETH II WITH PRINCE ANDREW AND PRINCE EDWARD. *Photograph by Cecil Beaton, 1964*

173. PRINCE CHARLES AND PRINCE EDWARD. *Still from a television film, 1969*

174. PRINCESS ANNE. *Press photograph, 1969*

175. PRINCESS ANNE. *Detail of a painting by Michael Noakes, 1973*

176. PRINCESS ANNE. *Photograph by Norman Parkinson, 1971*

Royal biographies & notes to the plates

Following the order of succession, each monarch is given a brief biography with dates of birth, death and reign. This is followed by a note on each portrait of that subject. The note gives details of the title, artist, plate number, medium, size, inscriptions, select exhibitions, bibliography and present owner, with a brief discussion of the more significant aspects of the portrait. Portraits of some consorts and other members of the royal family have also been included. The notes on these sometimes interrupt the sequence for an individual monarch as the notes are, where possible, arranged in the numerical order of the plates. The following abbreviations have been used:

EXH:	Exhibitions
LIT:	Literature
O. Millar, Tudor, Stuart	O. Millar, *The Tudor, Stuart and Early Georgian Pictures in the Collection of H.M. The Queen,* 2 vols, 1963
O. Millar, Later Georgian	O. Millar, *The Later Georgian Pictures in the Collection of H.M. The Queen,* 2 vols, 1969
Ormond	R. L. Ormond, *National Portrait Gallery: Early Victorian Portraits,* 2 vols, 1973
R. A.	Royal Academy
R. Strong, Elizabeth I	R. Strong, *Portraits of Queen Elizabeth I,* 1963
R. Strong, English Icon	R. Strong, *The English Icon: Elizabethan & Jacobean Portraiture,* 1969
R. Strong, NPG Cat.	R. Strong, *Tudor & Jacobean Portraits in the National Portrait Gallery,* 2 vols, 1969

WILLIAM I, 'THE CONQUEROR' (1027–87) *Reigned* 1066–87

Succeeded as Duke of Normandy, 1035. Invaded and conquered England, 1066, imposing on it a new feudal structure. Ordered a survey of his English possessions, embodied in Domesday Book, 1085. A great military leader and administrator.

William I. Detail from the Bayeux Tapestry *(Plate 3)*
Embroidery in wools on linen, 19¾ *in* × 230 *ft* 10¼ *in.*
Inscribed: HIC: WILLELM DVX: IVSSIT NAVES: EDIFICARE.
LIT: *Sir E. Maclagan,* The Bayeux Tapestry *(revised ed. 1953), Sir F. Stenton and others,* The Bayeux Tapestry *(revised ed. 1965), C. H. Gibbs-Smith,* The Bayeux Tapestry *(1973)*
Bayeux, Musée de la Tapisserie de la Reine Mathilde

The Bayeux Tapestry tells the story of the events leading to the Battle of Hastings in an elaborate narrative strip, packed with dramatic incidents. It is traditionally said to have been woven by William's queen, Matilda, but is now thought to have been commissioned by William's brother, Bishop Odo, from English craftsmen, possibly for his cathedral at Bayeux (dedicated in 1077), but more probably as a secular piece of decoration. The detail reproduced here shows William in conference with Bishop Odo giving orders for the construction of his invasion fleet.

William I. Seal by an Unknown Artist *(Plate 4)*
Wax seal, 3¼ *in diameter. Inscribed around rim of obverse:* [HOC. NORMANNORVM. WI]LLELMVM. NOSCE. PATRONUM. S[I.], *and of reverse:* HOC. ANGLIS. REGE[M. S]IGNO. [FATEARIS. EVNDEM.]. LIT: *W. de G. Birch,* Catalogue of Seals in the Department of Manuscripts in the British Museum, *I (1887), pp. 3–4 (15); A. B. and A. Wyon,* The Great Seals of England *(1887), pp. 5–6 (11 & 12)*
London, British Library, XXXIX. 8

An example of William I's first seal. He is shown on horseback on the obverse with lance and pennon, and enthroned with crown, sword and orb on the reverse or counter-seal.

William I. Coin by Ordric of Gloucester *(Plate 5)*
Silver penny, ¾ *in diameter. Obverse inscribed:* PILLEMVS REX I. LIT: *H. A. Grueber,* Handbook of the Coins of Great Britain and Ireland in the British Museum *(1899), p. 34 (198); G. C. Brooke,* Catalogue of English Coins in the British Museum: The Normans *(1916), II, p. 5 (16)*
London, British Museum

Crowned, with a sceptre. An example of type I of William's coinage.

WILLIAM II (*died* 1100) *Reigned* 1087–1100

Son of William I. Called 'Rufus' from his ruddy complexion. Antagonized his countrymen by his extortionate tax demands, and his cruelty. Undertook various inconclusive military campaigns in France. Shot while hunting, perhaps accidentally.

William II. Coin by Lifsun of Maldon *(Plate 6)*
Silver penny, ¾ *in diameter. Obverse inscribed:* PILLELM REX. LIT: *Grueber, op. cit., p. 35 (206); Brooke, op. cit., II, p. 220 (34)*
London, British Museum

Crowned, holding a sword. An example of type I of William II's coinage; there is some confusion between his coinage and that of his father.

HENRY I (1068–1135) *Reigned 1100–35*

Younger son of William I. Succeeded in containing the power of the barons, and extended royal administration in fiscal and financial matters. Reconquered many of the French territories held by his father, including Normandy. Secured the submission of the Welsh, and put down numerous rebellions in his possessions.

Henry I. Seal by an Unknown Artist *(Plate 7)*
Wax seal, 3⅜ in diameter. Inscribed around rim of obverse : HENRICVS DE [I] GRA[CI]A REX ANGLORVM, *and of reverse :* HENRICVS DEI GRATIA DVX NORMANNORVM. LIT : *Birch, op. cit., pp. 7–8 (31); Wyon, op. cit., p. 11 (23 & 24)*
London, British Library, Cott. Ch. VII. 2

Seated on a throne on the obverse, with sword and orb, and on horseback with lance, on the reverse or counter-seal.

Henry I. Coin by Wulfgar of London *(Plate 8)*
Silver penny, ¾ in diameter. Obverse inscribed : HENRIC REX. LIT : *Grueber, op. cit., p. 36 (212); Brooke, op. cit., II, p. 276 (34)*
London, British Museum

Crowned, holding a sceptre. An example of type 5 of Henry's coinage.

STEPHEN (?1097–1154) *Reigned 1135–54*

Son of William I's daughter, Adela. Though he had sworn to support Henry I's daughter, the Empress Matilda, he claimed the English throne and was chosen king. His reign was disturbed by constant civil war.

Stephen. Coin by William of Carlisle *(Plate 9)*
Silver penny, ¾ in diameter. Obverse inscribed : STEIFNE REX. LIT : *Grueber, op. cit., p. 37 (218); Brooke, op. cit., II, p. 337 (19)*
London, British Museum

Crowned, holding a sceptre. An example of type I of Stephen's coinage, and of notably coarser workmanship than the coins of his predecessors.

HENRY II (1133–89) *Reigned 1154–89*

Son of the Empress Matilda. Came to terms with Stephen, the usurper, and succeeded him. Instituted major reforms, aimed at increasing the power and efficiency of the Crown, and lessening its dependence on the feudal structure, arousing the hostility of the Church and barons. Crushed the Scots and Irish, and successfully defended his lands in France. Later came into conflict with his ambitious sons.

Henry II. Coin by Isaac of York *(Plate 10)*
Silver penny, ¾ in diameter. Obverse inscribed : HENRICVS REX. LIT : *Grueber, op. cit., p. 40 (231); G. C. Brooke, English Coins (revised ed., 1962), pp. 110–11*
London, British Museum

Crowned, holding a sceptre. An example of the short-cross issue introduced in 1180.

Henry II. Detail of effigy by an Unknown Artist *(Plate 12)*
Life-size stone effigy. LIT : C. A. Stothard, Monumental Effigies of Great Britain (1817); Abbé Edouard, Fontevrault et ses Monuments (1873); Archaeologia, LX (1907), p. 523; E. Panofsky, Tomb Sculpture (1964), p. 57 Maine-et-Loire, Abbey of Fontevrault

There is little doubt that this effigy represents the dead king as he was carried to his burial. Benedict of Peterborough records that he was 'clothed in royal apparel, wearing a golden crown on his head, and having gloves on his hands and a golden ring on his finger, a sceptre in his hand, footgear woven with gold, and spurs on his feet, girt with a sword'. The effigies of Henry, his queen (Eleanor of Aquitaine), Richard I *(Plates 13 and 14)* and Isabella (queen of John), are the earliest sculptures of English monarchs to survive *(see Plate 11)*. They were removed from the abbey at the time of the French Revolution, and thus escaped destruction, but they have suffered considerable damage.

RICHARD I (1157–99) *Reigned 1189–99*

Succeeded his father, Henry II. A born soldier, he spent most of his life campaigning abroad, leaving the realm in the hands of his brother, John, and loyal officials. He was the only English monarch to lead a crusade to the Holy Land.

Richard I. Effigy by an Unknown Artist *(Plates 13 and 14)*
Life-size stone effigy. LIT : As for Plate 12
Maine-et-Loire, Abbey of Fontevrault

Richard was buried at the feet of his father at his own wish. His effigy, like that of his father, shows him on a bier with crown and coronation ornaments as he was when carried to his burial.

JOHN (?1167–1216) *Reigned 1199–1216*

An ambitious figure, who resented his position as the youngest son of Henry II. Attempted to seize the English crown during the absence of his brother, Richard I, whom he succeeded. Lost many of his lands in France, and alienated all sections of English life by his oppressive rule. Forced to concede demands of barons at Runnymede, enshrined in Magna Carta, 1215.

John. Detail of effigy by an Unknown Artist *(Plate 15)*
Life-size marble effigy. LIT: *C. A. Stothard, op. cit.,; L. Stone,* Sculpture in Britain: the Middle Ages *(1955), pp. 105, 116*
Worcester Cathedral

The figure wears a dalmatic robe, jewelled gloves, and a crown on his head supported by two bishops. He holds a sword-hilt in one hand, and the handle of a sceptre in the other. Stothard records details of colour, possibly medieval in origin, which were obliterated when the tomb was gilded in 1873. The effigy was executed posthumously, probably between 1225–30, by an artist of the Purbeck school. In spite of its powerful effect, the head is almost certainly not a portrait. The effigy of John's queen, Isabella, is at Fontevrault (*see Plate 11*).

HENRY III (1207–72) *Reigned 1216–72*

Son of John. During his long reign, the power of the Crown was gradually eroded. Forced to make concessions to the barons, led by Simon de Montfort, and to the Pope. Lost many of his possessions abroad, and lost control of Wales.

Henry III. Effigy by William Torel *(Plates 16 and 18)*
Life-size bronze effigy. LIT: *L. Stone,* Sculpture in Britain: the Middle Ages *(1955), pp. 142–3; R. Strong, NPG Cat., I, p. 140*
London, Westminster Abbey

Commissioned with an effigy of Eleanor of Castile (*Plate 17*) by Edward I, 1291, no doubt in emulation of the French royal tombs in Saint-Denis. Torel, a London goldsmith, took two years to complete the figures, which were then cast in bronze.

EDWARD I (1239–1307) *Reigned 1272–1307*

Defeated de Montfort at Battle of Evesham, 1265. Won great prestige as crusader shortly before his accession, 1270. Succeeded his father, Henry III. Restored the authority of the Crown at the expense of the Church and barons. A great military leader, he defeated the Welsh and Scots in successive campaigns. Recovered many Plantagenet possessions in France.

Edward I. Seal by an Unknown Artist *(Plate 20)*
Wax seal, 4 in diameter. Inscribed around rim of obverse: EDWARDVS: DEI: [GRACIA: REX: ANGLIE:] DOMINVS: H[YBERNIE: DVX: AQVITANIE]. *Similar inscription on reverse.* LIT: *W. de G. Birch, B.M. Seals, op. cit., I, p. 20 (136); Wyon, op. cit., pp. 26–7 (47 & 48) London, British Library, Harl. Ch. 43 c. 52*

The king is shown on the obverse enthroned with orb and sceptre, and on horseback with sword and shield, on the reverse or counter-seal. The throne on the obverse is of elaborate tabernacle work, adorned with arcading. Underfoot are two small lions, and a further two are shown leaping up.

Edward I. Coin by an Unknown Artist *(Plate 21)*
Silver groat, $1\frac{1}{8}$ in diameter. Obverse inscribed: EDWARDVS: D'I: GRA': REX: ANGL'. LIT: *Grueber, op. cit., p. 44 (242); G. C. Brooke,* English Coins *(revised edition, 1962), p. 122 London, British Museum*

The groat, a coin worth four pence, was ordered in 1279, and the issue was probably of short duration.

ELEANOR OF CASTILE (*died 1290*)

Daughter of Ferdinand III of Castile. Married Prince Edward, later Edward I, 1254, and accompanied him on his crusade, 1270. Said to have saved his life by sucking a poisoned wound.

Eleanor of Castile. Detail of effigy by William Torel *(Plate 17)*
Life-size bronze effigy. LIT: *L. Stone, op. cit., pp. 142–3 London, Westminster Abbey*

Commissioned at the same time as the effigy of Henry III (*Plates 16 and 18*) in 1291. The image of the queen is probably derived from her seal, also by Torel.

EDWARD II (1284–1327) *Reigned 1307–27*

The first Prince of Wales. Succeeded his father, Edward I. Alienated the barons by pandering to favourites, especially Piers Gaveston. Disastrously defeated by Robert Bruce at Bannockburn, 1314. Dethroned by his wife, Isabella, with the support of her lover, Mortimer. Brutally murdered in Berkeley Castle.

Edward II. Tomb by an Unknown Artist
(Plates 19 and 22)
Life-size alabaster effigy. LIT: *L. Stone, op. cit., pp. 160–2*
Gloucester Cathedral

Commissioned in the 1330s by Edward III as a memorial to his father. It is one of a group of royal tombs executed at this period which are among the earliest and finest examples of alabaster carving in England. They were originally coloured and gilded.

EDWARD III (1312–77) *Reigned* 1327–77

Overthrew the rule of his mother, Isabella, and her lover, Mortimer, 1330. Restored political stability and the prestige of the monarchy. Responsible for an enlightened commercial policy and the resurgence of English naval power. Won a series of brilliant victories against the French at the beginning of the Hundred Years War.

Edward III. Detail of tomb effigy by an Unknown Artist *(Plate 23)*
Life-size copper gilt effigy. LIT: *L. Stone, op. cit., pp. 192–3; R. Strong, NPG Cat., I, pp. 84–5*
London, Westminster Abbey

Executed around 1377–80 and possibly based on the head of the funeral effigy *(Plate 24)*. It reflects the strong influence of French sculpture, already evident in the tomb effigy of Edward's queen, Philippa of Hainault, by Jean de Liège.

Edward III. Detail of funeral effigy attributed to Stephen Hadley *(Plate 24)*
Life-size wooden effigy. LIT: *Archaeologia, LX (1907), pp. 531–2 and XCVIII (1961), pp. 160–2; L. Stone, op. cit., pp. 192–3*
London, Westminster Abbey

According to the Wardrobe Account, Stephen Hadley was paid for 'an image in likeness of a king' soon after Edward's death. This was placed on the king's coffin in St Paul's prior to his burial. It seems likely that Hadley's image is the wooden effigy reproduced here, one of several surviving effigies of early English kings.

RICHARD II (1367–1400) *Reigned* 1377–99

Son of the Black Prince and grandson of Edward III. Succeeded as a minor. Won popularity by suppressing peasants' uprising led by Wat Tyler. Later alienated many of great nobles, and, after defeating their ringleaders, ruled harshly and autocratically. Defeated and deposed by exiled Duke of Lancaster (formerly Hereford), whom he had dispossessed.

Richard II. Painting by an Unknown Artist *(Plates 25 and 26, Plate 25 is from an infra-red photograph)*
Oil on panel, 84 × 43 in. EXH: *Kings and Queens, R. A. Winter, 1953 (51), with earlier literature.* LIT: *J. Evans, Oxford History of English Art (1949), pp. 101–2; Archaeologia, XCVIII (1961), p. 12 & n.; R. Strong, NPG Cat., I, p. 261*
London, Westminster Abbey

Various dates have been suggested for this interesting and unusual picture, but most authorities agree that it was executed during the king's lifetime. In spite of its idealized and hieratic qualities, it retains a sense of individual character.

Richard II presented to the Virgin and Child by his patron saints (the 'Wilton Diptych'). Detail of left-hand panel by an Unknown Artist *(Plate 27)*
Oil on two separate panels, each 18 × 11½ in (painted surface). LIT: *M. Davies, National Gallery Catalogues: French School (1957), pp. 92–101; Archaeologia, XCVIII (1961), pp. 1–28, both quoting extensive literature*
London, National Gallery

Opinions differ as to whether this picture was painted during the king's lifetime, or soon after his death as a memorial picture. It is the most important English painting of its period to survive, although its purpose and meaning remain obscure. As a likeness the portrait of Richard agrees reasonably well with the Westminster Abbey panel *(Plate 26)* and the tomb effigy there.

HENRY IV (1367–1413) *Reigned* 1399–1413

Son of John of Gaunt. As Duke of Hereford sent into exile after his quarrel with Thomas Mowbray, Duke of Norfolk. Dispossessed on the death of his father. Invaded England and defeated Richard II, whom he afterwards deposed. Spent most of his reign suppressing rebellions and securing his position.

Henry IV and Joanna of Navarre. Detail of effigies by an Unknown Artist *(Plate 29)*
Life-size alabaster effigies. LIT: *L. Stone, op. cit., p. 197; R. Strong, NPG Cat., I, p. 142*
Canterbury Cathedral

This joint tomb of Henry and his queen was probably executed between 1408 and 1427, when the chantry chapel was dedicated. When the tomb was opened in 1832, the head and beard of Henry's corpse were found to be remarkably well-preserved, and they proved that the effigy was a fairly accurate likeness.

HENRY V (1387–1422) *Reigned* 1413–22

Silenced disaffection at home by a war with France, winning a great victory at Agincourt, 1415. Extended his conquests in subsequent campaigns, and by the treaty of Troyes declared heir to Charles VI and regent of France.

Henry V. Miniature by an Unknown Artist *(Plate 28)*
Watercolour on vellum ; page size, $11\frac{3}{8} \times 7\frac{3}{8}$ *in ; miniature size,* $5\frac{1}{4} \times 4$ *in. From the presentation copy of Thomas Occleve's poem, 'De Regimine Principum'.* LIT : Catalogue of Manuscripts in the British Museum, part I, the Arundel Manuscripts (1840), *p.* 9; *M. Rickert,* Painting in Britain: the Middle Ages (1954), *p.* 185
London, British Library, Arundel MS 38

One of the most important likenesses of Henry executed during his lifetime. He is shown receiving a copy of Occleve's book from the author.

HENRY VI (1421–71) *Reigned* 1422–61 *and* 1470–1

Succeeded as a minor. Never able to contain the rivalries of certain powerful nobles. Lost many of his French possessions. Deposed by Edward, Duke of York, 1461. Briefly restored by the Earl of Warwick, 1470, but captured the following year and murdered. Noted for piety and learning.

Henry VI. Painting by an Unknown Artist *(Plate 31)*
Oil on panel, $22\frac{1}{4} \times 14$ *in. Inscribed later :* HENRY THE SIXTH. EXH : Richard III, *National Portrait Gallery,* 1973 (P4). LIT : *O. Millar,* Tudor, Stuart, I, *p.* 50 (8)
Her Majesty the Queen

The earliest known version of the standard portrait of Henry VI, included in sets of early kings and queens. It was presumably painted in the same workshop as Plates 32 and 34, and may be based on some lost image from the life.

EDWARD IV (1442–83) *Reigned* 1461–83

Leader of the powerful Yorkist faction. Defeated the Lancastrians and declared himself king, 1461. Forced into exile by Earl of Warwick, 1470, but defeated him the next year and firmly established his rule. An able and forward-looking administrator.

Edward IV in council. Miniature by an Unknown Artist *(Plate 30)*
Watercolour on vellum, $17\frac{3}{4} \times 13\frac{3}{4}$ *in. From Jean de Waurin's 'Premier volume des anchiennes et nouvelles Chroniques*

d'angleterre'. EXH : Richard III, *National Portrait Gallery,* 1973 (99). LIT : *G. F. Warner and J. P. Gilson,* Catalogue of Western Manuscripts in the Old Royal and King's Collections (1920), II, *p.* 176
London, British Library, Royal MS 15.E.IV

Jean de Waurin is presenting his chronicle to Edward, who is attended by various courtiers; the figure on the right in a long robe with the garter may be Richard III, and that on the left with the garter possibly Lord Hastings or Lord Rivers. The manuscript was executed in Flanders for Edward IV during his brief exile there in 1470–1. It includes twenty-nine large illuminations and a number of decorated borders.

Edward IV. Painting by an Unknown Artist *(Plate 32)*
Oil on panel, $26\frac{3}{4} \times 18\frac{7}{8}$ *in. Inscribed later :* K EDWARD YE 4TH. EXH : Richard III, *National Portrait Gallery,* 1973 (P8). LIT : *O. Millar,* Tudor, Stuart, I, *pp.* 50–1 (10)
Her Majesty the Queen

Of better quality than other portraits in this group (*Plates 31 and 34*), and possibly from life. There is a unique engraving that relates closely to this type of about 1472. Workshop versions are common.

EDWARD V (1470–83) *Reigned* 1483

Eldest son of Edward IV. Deposed by his uncle, Richard of Gloucester, and later murdered with his brother in the Tower.

Edward V when Prince of Wales. Stained glass by an Unknown Artist *(Plate 33)*
Stained glass window. Inscribed : EDWARDUS PRINCEPS WALLIE/PRIMUS FILIUS EDWARDI QUARTI.
LIT : *B. Rackham,* The Ancient Glass of Canterbury Cathedral (1949), *p.* 174 (H2)
Canterbury Cathedral

One of the lights in the North (Royal) Window of the north-west transept. This was given to the cathedral by Edward IV, and he and his family appear in it as donors. The window was damaged by iconoclasts in December 1643, and the arrangement of the glass is now significantly different. The figure of Edward V is original, but his face is a modern copy. He is shown kneeling at a low desk with a devotional book open in front of him. In the background is a curtain, part of it decorated with the prince's badge of a single ostrich feather, and a scroll inscribed with the motto *Ic dien* (I serve). According to Rackham, the window was almost certainly complete by the end of 1482, and it was probably painted in the studio of the king's glazier, William Neve, at Westminster.

RICHARD III (1452–85) *Reigned* 1483–5

Brother of Edward IV, and one of the most able Yorkist commanders. Deposed and possibly murdered his nephew, Edward V, and dealt ruthlessly with the Queen Mother's faction. Defeated and killed at the Battle of Bosworth by Henry Tudor, the Lancastrian claimant.

Richard III. Painting by an Unknown Artist *(Plate 34)*
Oil on panel, 22¼ × 14 in. EXH: Richard III, *National Portrait Gallery,* 1973 (P44). LIT: *O. Millar,* Tudor, Stuart, I, *p.* 51 (14)
Her Majesty the Queen

The earliest known version of a portrait of Richard, possibly from life, included in sets of early kings and queens. It was presumably painted in the same workshop as Plates 31 and 32. There is some hint of Richard's hunchback in the raised right shoulder, but an X-ray shows that the outline of the shoulder was originally lower.

HENRY VII (1457–1509) *Reigned* 1485–1509

Defeated and killed Richard III at Battle of Bosworth. After generations of civil war, established political stability and laid the foundations for the great achievements of the Tudor dynasty. Promoted commerce and learning, and pursued a successful policy of peace abroad. Instituted major reforms in every sphere of government.

Henry VII. Painting by Michel Sittow *(Plate 35)*
Oil on panel, 16¾ × 12 in. Inscribed: ANNO 1505 20 OCTOBRE YMAGO HENRICH VII FRANCIEGE REGE ILLUSTRUSSIMI ORDINATA F HERMANU RINCK RO REGIE . . . *[illegible]* MISSIARIUM. EXH: Kings and Queens, *R. A. Winter,* 1953 (64). LIT: *R. Strong,* NPG Cat., I, *pp.* 149–50
London, National Portrait Gallery

Painted during the marriage negotiations between the recently widowed Henry and Margaret of Savoy, daughter of the Emperor Maximilian. It was commissioned by the emperor's agent, Herman Rinck, and taken back to Margaret to show her the likeness of her intended husband. The marriage project was subsequently abandoned.

Henry VII. Bust attributed to Pietro Torrigiano *(Plate 36)*
Painted and gilded terracotta bust, 23⅞ in high. LIT: Journal of the Warburg and Courtauld Institutes, XIII (1950), *pp.* 222–4; Catalogue of Italian Sculpture in the Victoria and Albert Museum (1964), II, *pp.* 399–401
London, Victoria and Albert Museum

One of three similar terracotta busts first mentioned in 1779 as having been taken out of a room over the Holbein Gate, Whitehall (demolished in 1759). The other busts remain unidentified, but this one seems certainly to be Henry VII on the basis of comparison with other portraits. The similar treatment of features in the tomb effigy (*Plate 37*) supports the idea that it was sculpted by Torrigiano.

Henry VII. Detail of effigy by Pietro Torrigiano *(Plate 37)*
Life-size bronze effigy. LIT: Journal of the Warburg and Courtauld Institutes, XIII (1950), *p.* 221; *J. Pope-Hennessy,* Italian Renaissance Sculpture (*revised edition* 1971), *p.* 304; Archaeologia, XCVIII (1961), *pp.* 166–7; *M. Whinney,* Sculpture in Britain 1530 to 1830 (1964), *p.* 4; *R. Strong,* NPG Cat., I, *pp.* 150–1
London, Westminster Abbey

Torrigiano executed the effigies of Henry and his queen, Elizabeth of York, for their joint tomb between 1519–20. For the bust of Henry attributed to this artist, see Plate 36.

HENRY VIII (1491–1547) *Reigned* 1509–47

Son of Henry VII. A devotee of hunting, learning and the arts, he early on left government in the hands of Cardinal Wolsey. His military and diplomatic interventions in Europe emptied the exchequer and achieved little. Broke with the Pope over the question of his divorce from Catherine of Aragon, and declared himself supreme head of the English Church. With the aid of parliament carried through a radical legislative programme. The power of the Crown has perhaps never again been as great. Six wives.

Henry VIII. Painting attributed to Joos van Cleve *(Plate 38)*
Oil on panel, 28 × 22 in. Scroll inscribed with a passage from Gospel of St Mark. EXH: King's Pictures, *R. A. Winter,* 1946–7 (1). LIT: *R. Strong,* NPG Cat., I, *p.* 158
Her Majesty the Queen

The passage on the scroll is usually taken to refer to the publication of the English Bible in 1535. The portrait offers an interesting comparison to the Holbein of 1536 (*Plate 39*).

Henry VIII. Painting by Hans Holbein *(Plate 39)*
Oil and tempera on panel, 11 × 7½ in. EXH: Pictures from the Thyssen-Bornemisza Collection, *National Gallery,* 1961 (65); Erasmus, *Boymans Museum, Rotterdam,* 1969 (157). LIT: *P. Ganz,* The Paintings of Hans Holbein (1950), *p.* 248 (94); *R. Strong,* NPG Cat., I, *p.* 158, *and* Holbein and Henry VIII (1967), *p.* 37
Lugano, Thyssen-Bornemisza Collection

The only surviving painting of Henry certainly from Holbein's hand. It seems to have been painted soon after the king's marriage to Jane Seymour in 1536, and may once have formed part of a diptych recorded in an inventory of the king's pictures. Holbein made use of the same face pattern for the cartoon of his Whitehall fresco (*Plate 42*).

Henry VIII. Painting by an Unknown Artist after Hans Holbein *(Plate 40)*

Oil on canvas, 92 × 53 in. EXH: King and Queens, *Walker Art Gallery, Liverpool, 1953 (3).* LIT: *P. Ganz, op. cit., p. 289; R. Strong, NPG Cat., I, p. 159*
Liverpool, Walker Art Gallery

The earliest and best of several surviving copies of the figure of Henry in Holbein's fresco of 1536–7 (*see Plate 41*). It gives some idea of the overwhelming impact made by Holbein's original portrait. Another copy is signed by Hans Eworth, and it has been suggested that this one might also be from his hand.

Henry VII, Elizabeth of York, Henry VIII and Jane Seymour. Painting by Remigius van Leemput after Hans Holbein *(Plate 41)*

Oil on canvas, 35 × 38⅞ in. On the upper part of the sarcophagus or altar are some Latin verses in praise of the Tudors. Below is an inscription, signature and date, 1667. LIT: *O. Millar,* Tudor, Stuart, I, p. 117 (216); *R. Strong,* Holbein and Henry VIII (1967), pp. 35–7, 57
Her Majesty the Queen

A copy of Holbein's famous fresco of 1536–7 for the privy chamber, Whitehall Palace (now destroyed). Strong suggests that the fresco was placed above the throne, and that the altar in Leemput's copy represents an opening for a window in the original. This copy and another by the same artist at Petworth are the most complete record of Holbein's fresco.

Henry VIII. Detail of cartoon by Hans Holbein *(Plate 42)*

Black ink and watercolour washes on paper, mounted on canvas, 101½ × 54 in. LIT: *P. Ganz, op. cit., p. 289 (179); R. Strong, NPG Cat., I, pp. 153–5, and* Hans Holbein and Henry VIII (1967), pp. 37 ff.
London, National Portrait Gallery

A detail of the cartoon for the left-hand side of Holbein's fresco of 1536–7 in Whitehall (*see Plate 41*), showing Henry VIII and, behind him, his father, Henry VII. Although much worn the cartoon is a unique record of the lost fresco, and a superb work of art. Holbein used the cartoon to transfer his design to the wall, and the pin-pricks used in the process are still clearly visible on the surface of the cartoon.

The head is based on the same face pattern as the painting in the Thyssen-Bornemisza collection (*Plate 39*); this was subsequently altered to a full face view in the fresco, possibly as a result of fresh sittings.

CATHERINE OF ARAGON (1485–1536)

Youngest child of Ferdinand and Isabella of Spain. Henry VIII's first queen and mother of the future Mary I. Her failure to produce a male heir and Henry's infatuation with Anne Boleyn led to the famous divorce case. Her marriage declared null by Cranmer, 1533. Much sympathy was felt for her.

Catherine of Aragon. Painting by an Unknown Artist *(Plate 43)*

Oil on panel, 22 × 17½ in. LIT: *R. Strong, NPG Cat., I, p. 39*
London, National Portrait Gallery

The only authentic life-scale portrait of Henry's first queen. Another version is in the Museum of Fine Arts, Boston.

ANNE BOLEYN (1507–36)

Henry VIII's second queen. Secretly married to him in January 1533 and crowned later the same year. Gave birth to a daughter, the future Elizabeth I, but not to a son. Executed on a charge of treason for alleged adultery.

Anne Boleyn. Painting by an Unknown Artist *(Plate 44)*

Oil on panel, 21⅜ × 16⅜ in. Inscribed: ANNA BOLINA VXOR-HENRI-OCTA. LIT: *R. Strong, NPG Cat., I, pp. 5–6*
London, National Portrait Gallery

A workshop version of the standard portrait of Anne, perhaps part of a series of kings and queens.

JANE SEYMOUR (?1509–37)

Married Henry VIII as his third queen, 1536. Died soon after giving birth to the future Edward VI. Henry genuinely mourned her.

Jane Seymour. Detail of painting by Hans Holbein *(Plate 47)*

Oil and tempera on panel, 25½ × 16 in. LIT: *P. Ganz, op. cit., p. 249 (97)*
Vienna, Kunsthistorisches Museum

Closely related to the full-length figure of Jane Seymour in the lost fresco of 1536–7 in Whitehall Palace (*see Plate 41*). A half-length version, with a different costume, is in the Mauritshuis, The Hague, and there is a preliminary drawing in the Royal Library at Windsor.

ANNE OF CLEVES (1515–57)

Daughter of the Duke of Cleves. Married Henry VIII as a result of the negotiations for a Protestant alliance, 1540. Her marriage annulled soon afterwards, and thenceforward lived in retirement.

Anne of Cleves. Painting by Hans Holbein (*Plate 45*)

Oil and tempera on parchment, laid on canvas, $25\frac{5}{8} \times 19$ in. LIT: *A. B. Chamberlain, Hans Holbein the Younger (1913), II, pp. 177 ff.; P. Ganz, op. cit., p. 251 (107) Paris, Louvre*

Said to have been painted in July 1539 at Schloss Düren, the home of the Duke of Cleves, as a pre-marriage portrait.

CATHERINE PARR (1512–48)

Twice widowed. Married Henry VIII as his sixth wife, 1543, and outlived him. Tried to ameliorate her husband's harshness and cruelty.

Catherine Parr. Painting by an Unknown Artist (*Plate 46*)

Oil on panel, 30×25 in. Inscribed later: KATHARINE PARRE. EXH: Kings and Queens, *Walker Art Gallery, Liverpool, 1953 (8).* LIT: *R. Strong, NPG Cat., I, pp. 364–5 London, National Portrait Gallery*

The only portrait of Catherine Parr with any claims to authenticity. An attribution to William Scrots has been suggested.

The family of Henry VIII. Painting attributed to Lucas de Heere (*Plate 48*)

Oil on panel, 51×71 in. Inscribed: THE QUEEN TO WALSINGHAM THIS TABLET SENTE/MARKE OF HER PEOPLES AND HER OWNE CONTENTE. *Around the frame is a long explanatory verse.* EXH: Kings and Queens, *R. A. Winter, 1953 (69); Hans Eworth, National Portrait Gallery and Leicester, 1965–6 (39).* LIT: *R. Strong, Elizabeth I, p. 79 (82), and English Icon, p. 140 (95) From the collection at Sudeley Castle, Gloucestershire*

Painted around 1570 as a gift from Elizabeth to Sir Francis Walsingham, the well-known statesman.

Edward VI and the Pope. Painting by an Unknown Artist (*Plate 49*)

Oil on panel, $24\frac{1}{2} \times 35\frac{3}{4}$ in. Inscribed with various anti-papal slogans. EXH: The Elizabethan Image, *Tate Gallery, 1970 (9).* LIT: *R. Strong, NPG Cat., I, pp. 344–5 London, National Portrait Gallery*

An anti-papal allegory painted around 1548, when Cranmer ordered the destruction of all religious images (an inset scene shows a statue of the Virgin and Child being dismantled). Henry VIII on his deathbed points to his son as his heir. Members of the council are seated at the table, while below the figure of the Pope is shown crushed under the dais and an open copy of the Bible.

EDWARD VI (1537–53) *Reigned 1547–53*

Henry VIII's only surviving son. In spite of the care lavished on him, grew up frail and sickly. Ruled under the influence of powerful protectors, first the Duke of Somerset, later the Duke of Northumberland. His reign is notable for the advent of the English Reformation.

Edward VI when Prince Edward. Painting by Hans Holbein (*Plate 52*)

Oil and tempera on panel, $22\frac{1}{8} \times 17\frac{3}{8}$ in. Inscribed below are some Latin verses by the court poet Sir Richard Morison, apparently added later. LIT: *A. B. Chamberlain, Hans Holbein the Younger (1913), II, p. 164; P. Ganz, op. cit., p. 251 (105); R. Strong, NPG Cat., I, pp. 91–2 Washington, National Gallery of Art, Mellon Collection*

Almost certainly the picture presented by Holbein to Henry VIII as a new year's gift, 1539/40. A preliminary drawing is in the Royal Library, Windsor.

Edward VI. Painting attributed to William Scrots (*Plate 53*)

Oil on panel, $65\frac{3}{4} \times 35\frac{3}{4}$ in. Inscribed: KINGE EDWARD. 6. EXH: The Elizabethan Image, *Tate Gallery, 1970 (24).* LIT: *E. Auerbach, Tudor Artists (1954), pp. 77–8; O. Millar, Tudor, Stuart, I, p. 66 (49); R. Strong, NPG Cat., I, pp. 93–4, and English Icon, p. 71 (6) Her Majesty the Queen*

A good version of the only official portrait of Edward as king. The attribution of this type to Scrots rests on a payment to him in 1551/2 for two full-lengths of Edward, one of them sent abroad to the English ambassador in France. The version reproduced here belonged to the 1st Lord Lumley in 1590, and bears the cartellino of his collection.

MARY I (1516–58) *Reigned 1553–8*

Henry VIII's elder daughter by Catherine of Aragon. A passionate Roman Catholic, she attempted to stamp out all traces of the Reformation. Cemented an alliance with Spain by marrying Philip II, and restored papal power. Joined Spain in a war against France and lost Calais. Her persecution of Protestants aroused bitter hostility.

Mary I. Painting by Anthonis Mor *(Plates 54 and 55)*
Oil on panel, 43 × 33 in. Signed and dated : ANTONIS MOR FACIEBAT 1554. LIT : *H. Hymans,* Antonio Moro (1910), *pp. 76–7; P. Hendy,* European and American Paintings in the Isabella Stewart Gardner Museum (1974 *ed.*), *pp. 165–8; M. J. Friedlander,* Early Netherlandish Painting (*revised ed.*), XIII (1975), *p. 102 (352)*
Madrid, Prado

The most famous portrait of Mary by one of the leading court painters of the period. Mor worked almost exclusively for the Habsburgs, and he is said to have painted Mary for her prospective father-in-law, Charles V, being rewarded with a golden chain and a pension. No contemporary evidence for his visit survives, and it is not known whether Mary is depicted before or after her marriage in July 1554. Two other versions of comparable quality are in the Isabella Stewart Gardner Museum, Boston, and the collection of the Marquess of Northampton.

ELIZABETH I (1533–1603) *Reigned 1558–1603*

Henry VIII's younger daughter by Anne Boleyn. Her reign saw the return of political stability, the lessening of religious tension, the expansion of trade and empire, and an unparalleled flowering of literature and the arts. Parried the machinations of hostile Catholic powers, and, when war with Spain could be avoided no longer, crushed the Armada. One of the most brilliant and remarkable British monarchs.

Elizabeth I sitting in judgement of the Pope. Engraving by Pieter van der Heyden *(Plate 50)*
Engraving, 8¼ × 10 in. LIT : *R. Strong,* Elizabeth I, *p. 109 (14)*
London, British Museum

An anti-papal satire of 1584–5, inspired by Titian's *Diana and Callisto*. The queen, attended by four of the Dutch provinces, points at Pope Gregory XIII, unveiled by Time and Truth, who hatches out various eggs, including the Inquisition and the Massacre of St Bartholomew.

Elizabeth I and the three goddesses. Painting attributed to Hans Eworth *(Plate 51)*
Oil on panel, 27⅞ × 33¼ in. Signed and dated : 1569/HE (*in*

monogram), Latin inscription on the frame. EXH : Hans Eworth, *National Portrait Gallery and Leicester, 1965–6 (37).* LIT : *O. Millar,* Tudor, Stuart, I, *p. 69 (58); R. Strong,* Elizabeth I, *p. 79 (81);* English Icon, *p. 144 (96)*
Her Majesty the Queen

A revised version of the Judgement of Paris, in which Elizabeth confounds the goddesses, Juno, Pallas Athene and Venus, and keeps the golden apple herself as combining the virtues of all three. She emerges from an archway with two ladies-in-waiting, and there is a view of Windsor Castle in the background. The form of the monogram is different from that in other works by Eworth, and the style of the picture suggests a different artist.

Elizabeth I when Princess Elizabeth. Painting by an Unknown Artist *(Plate 56)*
Oil on panel, 42⅞ × 32⅛ in. Inscribed : ELIZABETHA/[?FILIA] REX/ANGLIAE. EXH : Holbein, *R. A. Winter, 1950 (144).* LIT : *O. Millar,* Tudor, Stuart, I, *p. 65 (46); R. Strong,* Elizabeth I, *p. 53 (1), and* English Icon, *p. 74 (11)*
Her Majesty the Queen

Probably painted for Henry VIII around 1546, and recorded in the possession of Edward VI in 1547. It is similar in style to a three-quarter-length portrait of Edward in the Royal Collection, and an attribution to William Scrots has been suggested for both pictures. The only recorded portrait of Elizabeth before her accession, it is of exceptionally fine quality.

Elizabeth I. Painting by an Unknown Artist *(Plate 57)*
Oil on canvas, 50½ × 40 in. LIT : *R. Strong,* Elizabeth I, *pp. 84–6 (100), and* English Icon, *p. 299 (304); E. Auerbach and C. K. Adams,* Paintings and Sculpture at Hatfield House (1971), *pp. 59–61 (51); F. Yates,* Astraea (1975), *pp. 216–19*
The Marquess of Salisbury

The so-called *'Rainbow portrait'* from the rainbow which the queen holds, an allusion to peace and the dawn of a new golden age. It is an idealized and symbolic portrait of Elizabeth, painted around 1600 but making use of an earlier face pattern. The complex allusions in the picture are discussed at length by Miss Yates. The portrait has been attributed to various Anglo-Flemish painters, including Isaac Oliver and Marcus Gheeraerts the Younger.

Elizabeth I. Painting attributed to George Gower *(Plates 58 and 59)*
Oil on panel, 44½ × 50½ in. LIT : *R. Strong,* Elizabeth I, *p. 74 (65)*
F. Tyrrwhitt-Drake

The finest version of the so-called *'Armada portrait'*, with views of the battle in the background (repainted in the seventeenth century). The face pattern may have appeared shortly before 1588, but there is little doubt that the victory against the Armada stimulated demand for a new portrait of the queen. There are good grounds for supposing that the type originated in the studio of Gower, Elizabeth's serjeant painter. Another good version is at Woburn Abbey, and a third is in the National Portrait Gallery.

Elizabeth I. Miniature by Nicholas Hilliard *(Plate 60)*
Watercolour on card, 2 × 1⅞ in (oval). Inscribed: ER *(crowned)* ANO DM. 1572./AETATIS SUAE 38. EXH: Hilliard and Oliver, *Victoria and Albert Museum*, 1947 (6) *(new ed.* 1971*);* The Elizabethan Image, *Tate Gallery*, 1970 (72). LIT: *E. Auerbach*, Nicholas Hilliard (1961), *p.* 290 (19); *R. Strong*, Elizabeth I, *p.* 89 (3), *and* NPG Cat., I, *p.* 101
London, National Portrait Gallery

The earliest known miniature of Elizabeth by Hilliard, and presumably the result of sittings recorded in his treatise on limning (*Walpole Society*, I, 1912, pp. 28–9). Hilliard, the greatest native-born English artist of the sixteenth century, was Elizabeth's official miniaturist, and produced several portraits of her.

Elizabeth I. Miniature by Isaac Oliver *(Plate 61)*
Watercolour on card, 2⅜ × 2⅛ in (oval). EXH: Hilliard and Oliver, *Victoria and Albert Museum*, 1947 (163) *(new ed.* 1971*);* The Elizabethan Image, *Tate Gallery*, 1970 (79). LIT: *E. Auerbach, op. cit., p.* 329 (247); *R. Strong*, Elizabeth I, *pp.* 92–4 (12)
London, Victoria and Albert Museum

An unfinished miniature and one of the few portraits to show Elizabeth's ageing appearance. The head is closely related to the engraving by Simon de Passe of 1592, and may be the source for it.

Elizabeth I. Miniature by Nicholas Hilliard *(Plate 62)*
Watercolour on vellum, 2⅜ × 2⅛ in. EXH. Hilliard and Oliver, *Victoria and Albert Museum*, 1947 (78) *(new ed.* 1971*).* LIT: *E. Auerbach, op. cit., p.* 310 (131); *R. Strong*, Elizabeth I, *p.* 95 (18)
London, Victoria and Albert Museum

A good example of the Hilliard 'Mask of Youth' face pattern current from about 1590 onwards. The *'Rainbow portrait'* (*Plate 57*) shows the same face pattern on a large scale.

Elizabeth I. Engraving by William Rogers *(Plate 63)*
Engraving, 15¼ × 10¼ in. LIT: *A. M. Hind*, Engraving in England in the 16th and 17th Centuries, I (1952), *pp.* 265–7; *R. Strong*, Elizabeth I, *p.* 114 (30)
London, British Museum

The figure is apparently based on the drawing by Isaac

Oliver in the Royal Library, Windsor. This is the only known impression of the first state of the print (Hind records four in all), and it was probably published in the last decade of Elizabeth's reign. In the cartouche below are verses praising the queen, 'Th' admired Empresse through the worlde applauded', and on either side are her emblems, the pelican and the phoenix.

JAMES I (1566–1625) *Reigned 1603–25*

Succeeded his mother, Mary Queen of Scots, as James VI of Scotland, and made Elizabeth's heir. Pursued policies of peace and conciliation at home and abroad, not altogether successfully. Increasing financial dependence on parliament was to prove fatal to Stuart claims to absolutism.

James I. Painting by John de Critz *(Plate 64)*
Oil on canvas, 79 × 46½ in. EXH: The Elizabethan Image, *Tate Gallery*, 1970 (174). LIT: *R. Strong*, NPG Cat., I, *p.* 179
Major J. More-Molyneux

A good version of the first official portrait of James as king, introduced around 1606. De Critz was paid for a full-length portrait of James in that year, and as serjeant painter he seems the most likely artist. The situation is confused because Marcus Gheeraerts the Younger is known to have painted portraits of James making use of the same face pattern. According to Sir Anthony Weldon, the king could never be persuaded to sit for his portrait, 'which is the reason for so few good peeces of him'. The jewel worn by James in his hat is the 'mirror of Great Britain', made for him in 1604 to symbolize the union of the kingdoms.

James I. Miniature by Nicholas Hilliard *(Plate 65)*
Watercolour on card, 1⅝ × 1⅜ in (oval). EXH: Hilliard and Oliver, *Victoria and Albert Museum*, 1947 (80) *(new ed.* 1971*);* Kings and Queens, *R. A. Winter*, 1953 (114). LIT: *E. Auerbach, op. cit., p.* 310 (135)
Her Majesty the Queen

Hilliard painted several miniatures of James I. This is a good example of the first type dating from about 1603–8; other versions are recorded.

James I. Miniature by John Hoskins *(Plate 66)*
Watercolour on vellum, 2¼ × 1¾ in (oval). EXH: British Portrait Miniatures, *Edinburgh*, 1965 (49); Van Dyck, *Queen's Gallery, Buckingham Palace*, 1968 (97); Age of Charles I, *Tate Gallery*, 1972 (194)
Her Majesty the Queen

Painted for Charles I from a portrait by Paul van Somer of 1618, probably to fill a gap in a frame of miniatures.

ANNE OF DENMARK (1574–1619)

Daughter of Frederick II of Denmark and Norway. Married James I by proxy, 1589. Showed great interest in court entertainments, especially masques, many of which she commissioned, and in the arts generally.

Anne of Denmark. Miniature by Isaac Oliver
(Plate 67)
Watercolour on vellum or card, $2\frac{1}{8} \times 1\frac{3}{4}$ in (oval). Signed in monogram: IO. EXH: Hilliard and Oliver, Victoria and Albert Museum, 1947 (183) (new ed. 1971). LIT: E. Auerbach, op. cit., p. 249; R. Strong, NPG Cat., I, p. 8
London, National Portrait Gallery

One of Oliver's most sensitive and beautiful miniatures of the queen, whose official miniaturist he was. The costume and hairstyle are unusually elaborate.

HENRY FREDERICK, PRINCE OF WALES (1594–1612)

Dazzled his contemporaries with his brilliant accomplishments. His death from typhoid was regarded as a national disaster.

James I and Henry, Prince of Wales. Engraving by William van de Passe (Plate 68)
Engraving, $11\frac{7}{8} \times 8\frac{1}{8}$ in. Inscribed: JAMES BY THE GRACE OF GOD KING OF GREAT BRITANNIE etc. HENRII BY Y GRA: OF GOD PRINCE OF WALES. Signed: WILH: PASSEUS FIGU: ET SCULPSIT and GEORG: FEAREBRAND EXCUDIT. A laudatory poem is printed below and the date 1621. LIT: A. M. Hind, Engraving in England in the 16th and 17th Centuries, II (1955), pp. 291–2 (10)
London, National Portrait Gallery

The second state of a print originally representing James I with Prince Charles, later Charles I. It was altered to commemorate Prince Henry who had died in 1612, although the figure remained identical. The de Passe family were leading engravers of the period.

Henry Frederick, Prince of Wales, and his friend, John, Lord Harrington of Exton, in the hunting field. Painting attributed to Robert Peake the Elder
(Plate 69)
Oil on canvas, $79\frac{1}{2} \times 58$ in. Inscribed: 1603/AE^{TE} 11 and AE^{TE} 9. LIT: O. Millar, Tudor, Stuart, I, p. 79; R. Strong, English Icon, p. 234 (201)
New York, Metropolitan Museum of Art, Joseph Pulitzer Bequest

Almost certainly Peake's first portrait of Prince Henry, whose principal painter he was. The picture is interesting as one of the first royal hunting groups, but it betrays Peake's limited powers of drawing and composition. Another version is in the Royal Collection.

CHARLES I (1600–49) Reigned 1625–49

Overshadowed as a child by Prince Henry, but grew up to become a great patron of the arts. Succeeded his father, James I. His belief in the divine right of kings led to a direct confrontation with parliament. His personal rule of eleven years (1629–40) finally ended by financial insolvency and war with Scotland. Extreme demands by the Long Parliament prepared the way for civil war (1642–5), Charles's defeat and his eventual execution.

Charles I when Prince of Wales. Engraving by Renold Elstrack (Plate 70)
Engraving, $10\frac{3}{8} \times 7\frac{3}{8}$ in. Signed: RENOLD ELSTRACK SCULP. Charles's titles are given in a cartouche upper left, and the Prince of Wales's feathers on the right. Below are verses in praise of the sitter. LIT: A. M. Hind, Engraving in England in the 16th and 17th Centuries, II (1955), pp. 168–9 (10)
London, British Museum

The first state of the print, dating from about 1614–15. Later states show a progressively older face. It is interesting to compare this stiff and stylized image with Van Dyck's equestrian portrait (Plate 75), though the theme of imperial leadership is common to both.

Charles I and Henrietta Maria departing for the chase. Painting by Daniel Mytens (Plates 71, 72 and 77)
Oil on canvas, $111 \times 160\frac{3}{4}$ in. LIT: O. Millar, Tudor, Stuart, I, p. 86 (120); R. Strong, Van Dyck: Charles I on Horseback (1972), pp. 70–1
Her Majesty the Queen

The king and queen are shown about to go hunting, attended by Jeffery Hudson, while a negro page brings up their horses. To symbolize their love a putto scatters roses over them. The composition dates from about 1630–2, and the figures at least appear to be from Mytens's hand. Two other versions are known.

Charles I. Painting by Gerard Honthorst (Plate 73)
Oil on canvas, $30 \times 25\frac{1}{4}$ in. EXH: Age of Charles I, Tate Gallery, 1972 (78). LIT: NPG Annual Report, 1965–6 (1967), pp. 26–7
London, National Portrait Gallery

One of the first genuinely informal royal portraits, and

almost certainly from the life. Honthorst visited England in 1628, when he painted the large *Apollo and Diana* (Hampton Court) for Charles I, who appears as Apollo in a pose closely related to the National Portrait Gallery portrait.

The five eldest children of Charles I. Painting by Sir Anthony van Dyck *(Plate 74)*

Oil on canvas, 64¼ × 78¼ *in. Signed and dated :* ANTHONY VAN DYCK EQUES FECIT,/1637. *Inscribed with the names and dates of birth of the five sitters.* EXH: Age of Charles II, *R. A. Winter,* 1960–1 (6); Van Dyck, *Queen's Gallery, Buckingham Palace,* 1968 (5); Age of Charles I, *Tate Gallery,* 1972 (105). LIT: *O. Millar,* Tudor, Stuart, I, *p.* 99 (152)
Her Majesty the Queen

The picture represents, from left to right, Princess Mary, James, Duke of York, Charles, Prince of Wales, Princess Elizabeth and Princess Mary. Van Dyck received a hundred pounds for the picture and it hung in the King's Breakfast Chamber at Whitehall. Along with the earlier group of Charles I's three eldest children by the same artist, it is one of the first group representations of royal children, and reflects the importance which Charles and Henrietta Maria attached to their family.

Charles I on horseback with Monseigneur de Saint Antoine in attendance. Painting by Sir Anthony van Dyck *(Plate 75)*

Oil on canvas, 145 × 106¼ *in. Dated :* 1633. EXH: King's Pictures, *R. A. Winter,* 1947 (96); Van Dyck, *Queen's Gallery, Buckingham Palace,* 1968 (9); Age of Charles I, *Tate Gallery,* 1972 (93). LIT: *O. Millar,* Tudor, Stuart, I, *pp.* 93–4 (143)
Her Majesty the Queen

Painted for the Long Gallery at St James's Palace, where it hung at the end of a long vista. Its powerful illusionistic effect made a deep impression. This type of equestrian design was first developed by Rubens in his portrait of the Duke of Lerma, and Van Dyck himself had made use of it for earlier pictures. Monseigneur de Saint Antoine had been sent to James I by Henry IV of France with a gift of six horses, and he subsequently became riding master and equerry to Charles I.

— — — — — — — — — — — — — — — — — — —

HENRIETTA MARIA (1609–69)

— — — — — — — — — — — — — — — — — — —

Daughter of Henry IV of France. Married Charles I by proxy, 1625. After a bad start, the marriage proved to be exceptionally happy. Helped to promote the brilliant arts and culture of the Caroline court. Influenced her husband in politics, and played an active part in the civil war.

Henrietta Maria. Miniature by John Hoskins *(Plate 78)*

Watercolour on vellum, 3½ × 3 *in.* EXH: Age of Charles I, *Tate Gallery,* 1972 (196); Samuel Cooper, *National Portrait Gallery,* 1974 (146)
Her Majesty the Queen

Painted for Charles I in 1632, and recorded by his librarian, Van der Doort: 'Don by the life by Haskins . . . with a white feather and in a white laced dressing about her breast in a blewish purple habbitt and Carnation sleeves.' The miniature bears the monogram of Samuel Cooper on the reverse, and it is tempting to attribute this exceptionally fine miniature to him; he worked in the studio of Hoskins, who was his uncle.

Henrietta Maria. Painting by Sir Anthony van Dyck *(Plates 76 and 79)*

Oil on canvas, 42¾ × 33⅞ *in.* EXH: Flemish Art, *R. A. Winter,* 1953–4 (224); Van Dyck, *Queen's Gallery, Buckingham Palace,* 1968 (6). LIT: *O. Millar,* Tudor, Stuart, I, *p.* 97 (147)
Her Majesty the Queen

Painted in 1632, and probably the first single portrait of Henrietta by Van Dyck. The pose of the figure is closely related to the double portrait of her and Charles I in the Archbishop's Palace at Kremsier. The single portrait, painted in delicate silvery tones, is one of Van Dyck's most sensitive and ravishing creations.

Charles I. Bust by François Dieussart or Dusart *(Plate 80)*

Marble bust, 34 *in high. Signed and dated :* C.R. 1636./F. DIEUSSART VALLON FECIT. EXH: Kings and Queens, *R. A. Winter,* 1953 (138); Age of Charles I, *Tate Gallery,* 1972 (236). LIT: Burlington Magazine, XCI (1949), *p.* 10
The Duke of Norfolk

Probably executed for Thomas, Earl of Arundel. It is more revealing as a portrait than Le Sueur's statues and busts, and, with the lost Bernini marble, is the only work in sculpture to come close to Van Dyck's elegance of representation. Dusart was a Low Country artist much employed by the House of Orange.

Charles I. Detail of statue by Hubert Le Sueur *(Plate 81)*

Bronze equestrian statue. Dated : 1633. LIT: Burlington Magazine, XCI (1949), *pp.* 9–10; *M. Whinney and O. Millar,* English Art 1625–1714 (1957), *p.* 118
London, facing down Whitehall

The most famous sculpture of Charles I, commissioned by Richard Weston, Earl of Portland. Like Van Dyck's equestrian portrait (*Plate 75*), it recreates the martial and imperial imagery of antiquity. It was sold by the Puritans to be melted down for scrap, but the brazier, Rivett, who bought it, buried it in his garden and produced it uninjured at the Restoration. Le Sueur was responsible for several bronze busts of the king.

Charles I in three positions. Painting by Sir Anthony van Dyck (*Plates 82 and 83*)
Oil on canvas, 33¼ × 39¼ *in.* EXH. *Flemish Art, R. A. Winter*, 1953–4 (138); *Van Dyck, Queen's Gallery, Buckingham Palace*, 1968 (11); *Age of Charles I, Tate Gallery*, 1972 (86). LIT: *O. Millar*, Tudor, Stuart, 1, *pp.* 96–7 (146)
Her Majesty the Queen

Probably begun in the second half of 1635, and sent to Bernini in Rome to help in the execution of his bust of Charles I. The latter had been commissioned by the queen, and it was lavishly praised on its arrival in England in 1637; it was apparently destroyed in the Whitehall Palace fire of 1698. Van Dyck's design may have been influenced by Lorenzo Lotto's *Portrait of a man in three positions*, then owned by Charles I, and in turn it served as a model for triple portraits by later artists.

Charles I with his son, James, Duke of York. Painting by Sir Peter Lely (*Plate 84*)
Oil on canvas, 49¾ × 57¾ *in.* EXH: *Age of Charles II, R. A. Winter*, 1960–1 (4); *Noble Patronage, Hatton Gallery, Newcastle*, 1963 (23). LIT: *R. B. Beckett*, Lely (1951), *p.* 39 (78); *M. Whinney and O. Millar*, English Art 1625–1714 (1957), *pp.* 170–1; *E. K. Waterhouse*, Painting in Britain 1530 to 1790 (1969 *ed.*), *p.* 59
The Duke of Northumberland

The king holds a letter inscribed *Au Roy/Monsignor*, which he is about to open with a penknife handed to him by his son. The portrait was commissioned in 1647 by the Earl of Northumberland, who had the king's children in his charge. It was probably painted at Hampton Court where Charles I was held at that time. It inspired a famous poem by Lovelace, beginning with the lines, 'See! what a *clouded majesty,* and eyes/Whose glory through their mist doth brighter rise!' Among other pictures commissioned from Lely by the earl was a group of three royal children.

Charles I at his trial. Painting by Edward Bower (*Plate 85*)
Oil on canvas, 53 × 40¾ *in. Signed and dated:* EDW. BOWER./ATT TEMPLE BARR./FECIT 1648. EXH: *Age of Charles II, R. A. Winter*, 1960–1 (1); *Samuel Pepys, National Portrait Gallery*, 1970–1 (36). LIT: *Burlington Magazine*, XCI (1949), *pp.* 18–21; *O. Millar*, Tudor, Stuart, 1, *pp.* 114–15
Sir John Carew Pole, Bart

One of four signed and dated variants showing Charles I at the time of his trial. They were presumably worked up from studies made on the spot in Westminster Hall. This portrait is said to have been commissioned by John Carew, one of the judges who signed Charles I's death warrant. Little is known about Bower, whose work is provincial.

The execution of Charles I. Engraving by an Unknown Artist (*Plate 86*)
Engraving, 10¼ × 11¼ *in. Various inscriptions in German, identifying the subject and the chief participants, with the date 1649*
London, National Portrait Gallery

One of a number of popular prints of the execution, current in Europe at the time.

Charles I. Engraving by William Marshall (*Plate 87*)
Engraving, 6¼ × 6¾ *in. Signed:* GUIL: MARSHALL SCULPSIT. LIT: *M. Corbett and M. Norton*, Engraving in England in the 16th and 17th Centuries, III (1964), *pp.* 148–51 (154)
London, National Portrait Gallery

One of eight versions of a well-known design, executed originally as the frontispiece to *Eikon Basilike—The Pourtraicture of His Sacred Maiestie in his solitudes and sufferings* (1648), a book certainly inspired by Charles I, and probably in part written by him. He is shown in Marshall's print kneeling at prayer, holding a crown of thorns, and looking up at a heavenly diadem, while his temporal crown lies at his feet. The book in front of him is inscribed, 'IN VERBO TUO SPES MEA' (In Thy word is my hope); on the left is a rock amid heaving billows below the inscription, 'IMMOTA TRIUMPHANS' (Unshaken and triumphant); and a palm tree hung with weights and a scroll bearing the inscription, 'CRESCIT SUB PONDERE VIRTUS' (Virtue grows under burdens).

CHARLES II (1630–85) *Reigned* 1660–85

Defeated in the second civil war, 1650–1, and thereafter in exile. Restored to the throne two years after the death of Cromwell. His court noted for its extravagance and hedonism. Attempted to restrain the royalist backlash against the Puritans with little success. Financial problems brought him into conflict with parliament. Pursued a weak foreign policy, becoming the pensioner of Louis XIV of France. Famous for the number and beauty of his mistresses.

The Great Feast the Estates of Holland made to the king and to the royal family. Engraving by Pierre Philippe after Jacob Toorenvliet (*Plate 88*)
Engraving, 15¾ × 18⅝ *in. Signed by the artist and engraver.*

EXH: Samuel Pepys, *National Portrait Gallery*, 1970–1 (32). *From a set of plates illustrating* A Relation of the Voiage and Residence which Charles the II . . . hath made in Holland, from the 25 of May to the 2 of June, 1660, *translated by Sir William Lower (The Hague, 1660)*
London Library

Charles II was liberally entertained by the Dutch government prior to his departure for London.

The ball at The Hague. Detail of painting by Hieronymus Janssens *(Plate 89)*
Oil on canvas, $54\frac{1}{2} \times 85$ *in. Signed:* H. JANSSENS FECIT.
EXH: Charles II, *National Portrait Gallery*, 1960 (5); Age of Charles II, *R. A. Winter*, 1960–1 (48). LIT: *C. H. Collins Baker*, Catalogue of the Principal Pictures . . . at Windsor Castle (1937), *p.* 178
Her Majesty the Queen

The scene depicted is apparently a ball given at The Hague in May 1660 in honour of Charles II, shortly before his return to England. He is shown dancing with his sister, Mary, Princess of Orange. The seated figure immediately behind Charles is his brother, James, Duke of York, later James II, and the boy standing between the two ladies is Mary's son, the future William III. The artist specialized in scenes of this kind, and was known as 'Janssens der Danser'.

Charles II. Miniature by Samuel Cooper *(Plate 90)*
Watercolour on vellum, $6\frac{1}{2} \times 5\frac{1}{4}$ *in (oval). Signed and dated:* 1665/SC. EXH: Age of Charles II, *R. A. Winter*, 1960–1 (562); Samuel Cooper, *National Portrait Gallery*, 1974 (112)
The Hague, Mauritshuis

One of Cooper's finest miniatures of Charles II, and unusually large and elaborate. Another similar version is at Goodwood. Both show Charles II in garter robes. Cooper was appointed king's limner sometime before 1663, and he remained the leading English miniaturist until his death in 1672.

– – – – – – – – – – – – – – – – – – – –

CATHERINE OF BRAGANZA (1638–1705)
– – – – – – – – – – – – – – – – – – – –

Daughter of the king of Portugal. Married Charles II, 1662. Played little part in public affairs, and very much overshadowed by her husband's mistresses.

Catherine of Braganza. Miniature by Samuel Cooper *(Plate 91)*
Watercolour on vellum, $4\frac{7}{8} \times 3\frac{7}{8}$ *in (oval).* EXH: Kings and Queens, *R. A. Winter*, 1953 (191); Samuel Cooper, *National Portrait Gallery*, 1974 (79)
Her Majesty the Queen

This unfinished miniature is one of Cooper's most enchant-

ing works. It remained with the artist, and is thought to have been purchased from Cooper's widow by Charles II.

Charles II. Bust by Honoré Pelle *(Plate 92)*
Marble bust, 51 *in high. Signed and dated:* 1684 HONORE PELLE F. EXH: Charles II, *National Portrait Gallery*, 1960 (20); Age of Charles II, *R. A. Winter*, 1960–1 (445). LIT: Architectural Review, *August* 1913, *pp.* 33–4
London, Victoria and Albert Museum

Another version of the bust dated 1682 is at Burghley. Pelle was a French sculptor, who worked largely in Italy. No other busts of English subjects by him are known.

Charles II. Painting attributed to Hendrik Dankerts *(Plate 93)*
Oil on canvas, $36 \times 36\frac{3}{4}$ *in.* EXH: Charles II, *National Portrait Gallery*, 1960 (10). LIT: *H. Walpole*, Description of Strawberry Hill, 1784; *R. Edwards*, Early Conversation Pictures (1954), *pp.* 160–1; *O. Millar*, Tudor, Stuart, I, *pp.* 136–7
The Marchioness of Cholmondeley

The so-called '*Pineapple portrait*', showing the royal gardener, John Rose, presenting a pineapple to his patron. Walpole suggests that this was the first home-grown example, but it is more likely to have been imported. The house in the background is traditionally identified as Dorney Court in Buckinghamshire, but is probably Dorney House near Oatlands Park in Surrey. The costume suggests a date of *post* 1670. Dankerts, a Dutch artist specializing in views, may have painted the background, but is unlikely to have done the figures. A number of his landscapes are in the Royal Collection, which also contains another version of the '*Pineapple portrait*'.

Charles II. Painting by Sir Peter Lely *(Plate 94)*
Oil on canvas, $91\frac{1}{2} \times 56\frac{3}{4}$ *in.* EXH: Kings and Queens, *R. A. Winter*, 1953 (173); Charles II, *National Portrait Gallery*, 1960 (9); Age of Charles II, *R. A. Winter*, 1960–1 (64). LIT: *R. B. Beckett*, Lely (1951), *p.* 39 (81)
The Duke of Grafton

Probably the original of a very popular state portrait of about 1675. It may have been given by Charles II to the Duchess of Cleveland, whose eldest son by Charles became the first Duke of Grafton. The king is shown in garter robes, with the regalia on a table beside him. A similar face pattern was used for other designs produced in Lely's studio, and there are a number of related engravings.

JAMES II (1633–1701) *Reigned 1685–8*

Won distinction as a naval commander when Duke of York. Became a Roman Catholic, about 1670, and nearly excluded from the succession as a result. Succeeded his brother Charles II. Alienated his subjects by his attempts to reintroduce Catholicism and absolute monarchy. Forced into exile by Whig magnates, who offered the crown to William and Mary.

James II when Duke of York. Miniature by Samuel Cooper *(Plate 95)*
Watercolour on vellum, 2½ × 2⅛ in (oval). Signed and dated: SC/167– *(last numeral illegible).* EXH: Samuel Cooper, *National Portrait Gallery, 1974 (131)*
Greenwich, National Maritime Museum

Cooper died in May 1672, so the miniature must date from the first two years of the decade. Several other miniatures of James II by him are known, including one of 1661 in the Victoria and Albert Museum. The present one shows James in armour with the sash of the garter.

James II. Painting by Nicholas de Largillière *(Plate 96)*
Oil on canvas, 30 × 25 in. LIT: National Maritime Museum Catalogue of Portraits (1961), *p. 70*
Greenwich, National Maritime Museum

The best-known version of a portrait engraved in 1686. The gold-embossed armour worn by James II includes emblems of his various kingdoms. Largillière, a French artist, had worked for a time in Lely's studio, and he returned soon after James's accession to paint this portrait. He is said to have been subsequently driven out of England by the jealousy of his rivals.

James II. Painting by Sir Godfrey Kneller *(Plate 97)*
Oil on canvas, 92¾ × 56¾ in. Signed and dated: G. KNELLER FE./1684. EXH: Kings and Queens, R. A. Winter, 1953 (195); Sir Godfrey Kneller, *National Portrait Gallery, 1971 (91).* LIT: *D. Piper,* Catalogue of Seventeenth-Century Portraits in the National Portrait Gallery (1963), *pp. 176–7*
London, National Portrait Gallery

The painting originally depicted James as lord high admiral, shortly before his accession. The regalia were apparently added later, to update the picture. Behind James is an anchor, and beyond a man-of-war, presumably his flagship, firing a broadside. This is Kneller's most distinguished portrait of James, and there are a number of dependent copies and versions.

WILLIAM III (1650–1702) *Reigned with* MARY II, *1688–94, and on his own, 1694–1702*

Prince of Orange and Charles I's grandson. Invited to invade England, 1688, and crowned with his wife, Mary II. Devoted his life to resisting ambitions of Louis XIV, and led the Grand Alliance in a defensive war, 1689–97. At the time of his death planning a new alliance against the French.

William III. Painting by Godfried Schalcken *(Plate 98)*
Oil on canvas, 29½ × 24½ in. EXH: Kings and Queens, *Walker Art Gallery, Liverpool, 1953 (26).* LIT: *A. Staring, 'De Portretten van den Koning Stadhouder',* Nederlandisch Kunsthistorisch Jaarboek, III *(1952), pp. 186–7*
Shropshire, Attingham Park, National Trust

Schalcken, a Dutch painter famous for his light effects, came to England briefly in 1692. His candlelight portraits created a sensation, and Walpole records an anecdote that William himself held the candle until the tallow ran down his fingers. However, the head in Schalcken's portrait relates closely to the state portrait by Kneller of 1690, and it is unlikely to have been from life. Another signed version is in the Rijksmuseum, Amsterdam.

William III. Bust by Jan Blommendael *(Plate 99)*
Marble bust, 31½ in high. Signed and dated: J. BLOMMENDAEL F. HAGAE.COMITIS/1699. EXH: De Stadhouder-Koning, *Rijksmuseum, Amsterdam, 1950 (576);* William & Mary, *Arts Council, 1950 (93).* LIT: *A. Staring, op. cit., pp. 190–1 (20)*
The Hague, Mauritshuis

Presumably executed at The Hague, where the artist was resident. William was in Holland from 31 May to 18 October 1699, negotiating the second partition treaty. This florid baroque image of William, in robes of state with the garter collar, offers an interesting contrast to the more restrained representations of him by English artists.

William III. Detail of effigy, without wig, attributed to Mrs Goldsmith *(Plate 100)*
Effigy, with wax head, 66½ in high. LIT: *L. E. Tanner and J. L. Nevinson, 'On Some Later Funeral Effigies in Westminster Abbey',* Archaeologia, LXXXV *(1936), pp. 190–2; A. Staring, op. cit., pp. 192–5 (21)*
London, Westminster Abbey

One of a remarkable group of late seventeenth and early eighteenth-century effigies. Those of Charles II and members of his circle were made in connection with their funerals. A later group, including the effigies of William III and Mary II *(Plate 101)*, were added later to enhance the interest of the collection. The minor officials of the abbey supplemented their stipends by showing the effigies to the public for a small fee; the effigies of William and Mary were first exhibited on 1 March 1725. The head and hands of the effigy of William are made of wax, the body and legs of canvas and other materials. His costume, including the coronation mantle, is contemporary. The remarkably lifelike head, probably based on a death mask, may have been modelled by Mrs Goldsmith, who is known to have made the effigy of the Duchess of Richmond.

MARY II (1662–94) *Reigned with* WILLIAM III, 1688–94

Eldest daughter of James, Duke of York, later James II. Remained a Protestant, and married William of Orange, 1677. Accepted English crown with her husband, after the overthrow of her father. Owing to her husband's frequent campaigns abroad, played an active role in government.

Mary II. Effigy attributed to Mrs Goldsmith
(*Plate 101*)
Head, bust and hands of wax, the body of canvas stuffed with tow and stiffened with a wooden post and with wire, the legs similarly stuffed, 71 in high. LIT: *L. E. Tanner and J. L. Nevinson, op. cit., pp.* 190–4
London, Westminster Abbey

One of a group of effigies discussed in the note to Plate 100. The state robes worn by Mary, like those on the other effigies, are contemporary and constitute one of the most complete and important survivals of their kind.

ANNE (1665–1714) *Reigned* 1702–14

Second daughter of James, Duke of York, later James II, and sister of Mary II. Married Prince George of Denmark, 1683, but lost all her many children by him in infancy. Supported Marlborough in the War of the Spanish Succession, but later dismissed him, and allowed a Tory government to replace the Whigs.

Queen Anne. Painting by Edmund Lilly (*Plate 102*)
Oil on canvas, 81 × 56 in. Signed and dated: E. LILLY
FECIT. 1703. LIT: *G. Scharf,* Blenheim Palace Catalogue
(1862 *ed.*), *p.* 18; *E. K. Waterhouse,* Painting in Britain
1530 to 1790 (1969 *ed.*), *p.* 96
Oxfordshire, Blenheim Palace, by courtesy of His Grace the Duke of Marlborough

Lilly is an obscure artist, possibly of Norfolk origin. He evidently enjoyed considerable royal patronage under Queen Anne, painting at least two other portraits of her. The one reproduced here is the largest and most monumental. It is a surprisingly accomplished work, painted in cool, silvery tones.

GEORGE I (1660–1727) *Reigned* 1714–27

Son of Ernest Augustus of Hanover, and great grandson of James I. Took part in the Grand Alliance against Louis XIV. Succeeded Queen Anne who had died childless. Spoke almost no English, and took little interest in the affairs of his new kingdom.

George I. Painting by Sir James Thornhill (*Plate 103*)
Part of the decoration of the Queen's Bedchamber. LIT:
E. Croft-Murray, Decorative Painting in England
1537–1837, I (1962), *pp.* 269–70 (20)
Hampton Court, Her Majesty the Queen

The cove below the ceiling of the Queen's Bedchamber is decorated with four oval portraits of George I and members of his family, each held up by cupids, with slaves supporting swags in the corners. The regalia is shown on a cushion in front of George I, while a figure above holds out a laurel wreath. The portrait of the king relates closely to Kneller's state portrait of 1714, although in reverse. The decoration of the bedchamber was carried out by Thornhill between 1714 and 1715.

George I. Bust by Michael Rysbrack (*Plate 104*)
Marble bust, approx. 24¾ *in high. Signed:* M. RYSB^K FECIT.
LIT: *Mrs R. Lane Poole,* Catalogue of Oxford Portraits, III
(1925), *p.* 50 (127); *M. I. Webb,* Michael Rysbrack (1954),
pp. 179, 216
Oxford, Christ Church

George I is shown in elaborately decorated armour, with a laurel wreath in his hair, like a classical emperor. Other related versions are recorded, but a comment by George Vertue in 1732 about a marble bust of George I by Rysbrack, suggests that he may not have sat for them (*Walpole Society,* XXII, 1933–4, *p.* 56). Rysbrack, a native of Antwerp, was the most distinguished sculptor working in England in the early eighteenth century.

GEORGE II (1683–1760) *Reigned* 1727–60

Spent his early life in Hanover, and remained German in his outlook and attitudes. Like his father, George I, continued to support the Whigs, and interfered relatively little in domestic affairs. He was the last British sovereign to command in the field, at the Battle of Dettingen, 1743.

FREDERICK, PRINCE OF WALES (1707–51)

Like all Hanoverians got on notoriously badly with his father, George II, and led the opposition to him. Stamped his influence on contemporary taste by his discerning patronage of artists and designers. A keen musician, and one of the greatest of royal collectors.

Frederick, Prince of Wales, and his sisters. Painting by Philip Mercier (Plate 105)

Oil on canvas, 17¾ × 22¾ in. Signed and dated : PH. MERCIER FECIT/1733. EXH : Philip Mercier, *City Art Gallery, York, and Kenwood, London, 1969 (24). LIT : J. Kerslake, forthcoming catalogue of Georgian Portraits in NPG London, National Portrait Gallery*

The picture, one of three versions, shows Anne, Princess Royal, playing the harpsichord on the left, Princess Caroline playing the mandora, Frederick playing the cello, and Princess Amelia on the right reading a copy of Milton's poems. They are posed in front of the Dutch House, Kew, Anne's residence before her marriage. The French-born Mercier was librarian and principal painter to Frederick, and he painted the prince on a number of occasions.

George II. Painting by John Shackleton (Plate 106)

Oil on canvas, 93 × 56¼ in. Inscribed : HIS MAJESTY KING GEORGE THE SECOND SHACKLETON PINXIT. LIT : *B. Nicolson and J. Kerslake*, Treasures of the Foundling Hospital *(1972), pp. 32, 34, 50, 78 (74) London, Thomas Coram Foundation for Children*

Presented to the Foundling Hospital by the artist, 1758, in the same year that he was elected a governor. Shackleton was principal painter to George II from 1749.

George II. Caricature by George, 1st Marquess Townshend (Plate 107)

Ink on paper, 3⅛ × 2⅝ in. Inscribed in shorthand : T.K. LIT : *E. Harris*, The Townshend Album *(1974), p. 7 (2) London, National Portrait Gallery*

From an album of caricatures by Townshend, an influential political figure, and one of the first English caricaturists. Though hostile to the king, Townshend treats him quite mildly, and, to judge from other portraits, the likeness is surprisingly good.

George II. Bust by Louis François Roubiliac (Plate 108)

Marble bust, 31 in high. Signed : L.F. ROUBILIAC INV.ᵗ EXH : English Taste in the Eighteenth Century, *R. A. Winter, 1955–6 (216). LIT : K. A. Esdaile, The Life and Works of L. F. Roubiliac (1928), p. 91 Her Majesty the Queen*

A superb bust of the king in later life, apparently made without sittings. He is dressed in armour with the George of the Order of the Garter, a large lace cravat, and a flamboyant piece of drapery knotted at the side.

GEORGE III (1738–1820) *Reigned 1760–1820*

Eldest son of Frederick, Prince of Wales. Succeeded his grandfather, George II. Played an active but not always sensible part in politics. His obstinacy helped to provoke the American colonies and led to the War of Independence. Supported the younger Pitt, and showed great tenacity during the Napoleonic wars. After several breakdowns, became permanently insane, 1811. A patriotic and popular monarch.

George III. Painting by Allan Ramsay (Plate 109)

Oil on canvas, 98 × 64 in. EXH : Allan Ramsay, R. A. Winter, 1964 (51). LIT : A. Smart, Ramsay (1952), pp. 119–24; O. Millar, Later Georgian, I, pp. 93–4 (996) Her Majesty the Queen

Almost certainly the original version of Ramsay's first state portrait of George III, painted soon after his accession in October 1760; the king is dressed in coronation robes. So popular was this portrait, and a companion one of Queen Charlotte, that it was more copied than the state portrait of any other monarch. Ramsay was George III's favourite portraitist, and he was appointed principal painter in succession to Shackleton.

George III. Painting by Allan Ramsay (Plate 110)

Oil on canvas, 25 × 23 in. Inscribed : KING GEORGE III. LIT : *A. Smart, op. cit., pp. 111, 124 Private Collection*

Painted at the same period as Plate 109, as a profile image for the coinage.

George III. Bust by Agostino Carlini (Plate 111)

Marble bust, 31 in high. Inscribed : A. CARLINI F. 1773. EXH : British Portraits, *R. A. Winter, 1956–7 (517). LIT : M. Whinney, Sculpture in Britain 1530 to 1820 (1964), p. 141 London, Royal Academy of Arts*

Little is known about the sculptor, who came from Genoa. The bust of George III, one of the few recorded works by him, is a vigorous characterization.

George III and Queen Charlotte. Medallions by Samuel Percy (Plate 112)

Wax medallions, each 4⅛ × 2⅞ and 2½ in respectively. Inscribed on the back : MODELLED BY PIERCY, 1795.

LIT: *E. J. Pyke,* Biographical Dictionary of Wax Modellers (1973), *p.* 103
Her Majesty the Queen

Presumably a repetition of an earlier design. Percy was modelling waxes in high relief rather than in profile by the 1790s, and the appearance of the sitters points to a considerably earlier date.

QUEEN CHARLOTTE (1744–1818)

Youngest daughter of Charles Louis, brother of Frederick of Mecklenburg-Strelitz. Married George III, 1761. A devoted wife and the mother of a large family.

Queen Charlotte with her two eldest sons. Painting by Johann Zoffany *(Plate 113)*
Oil on canvas, $44\frac{1}{4} \times 50\frac{7}{8}$ *in.* EXH: George III, *Queen's Gallery, Buckingham Palace,* 1974 (18). LIT: *O. Millar,* Later Georgian, I, *p.* 149 (1199)
Her Majesty the Queen

Probably painted around 1765. The queen is shown at her dressing table, apparently in one of the new rooms on the garden front of Buckingham Palace. Prince Frederick, later Duke of York, is shown on the left in oriental costume, and Prince George, later Prince of Wales, in Roman costume on the right. Zoffany, a German artist, painted several family and other groups for George III.

GEORGE IV (1762–1830) *Reigned 1820–30*

Appointed Prince Regent after his father's final breakdown, 1811. His extravagance and dissolute private life were the subject of continuous scandal. A great collector and patron of art, and the moving spirit behind the Regency style which he did so much to promote.

A voluptuary under the horrors of digestion. Caricature by James Gillray *(Plate 114)*
Coloured etching, $13\frac{1}{4} \times 10\frac{3}{4}$ *in.* LIT: *M. D. George,* Catalogue of Political and Personal Satires in the . . . British Museum, VI (1938), *pp.* 920–1 (8112); *D. Hill,* Fashionable Contrasts: Caricatures by James Gillray (1966), *p.* 163 (56)
London, National Portrait Gallery

One of Gillray's most brilliant caricatures of the Prince of Wales, published on 2 July 1792. There are allusions to the prince's gluttony, his debts and his loose living; two of the medicines shown in the background are patent remedies for venereal disease.

George IV when Prince of Wales. Painting by Sir Joshua Reynolds *(Plate 115)*
Oil on canvas, $94\frac{1}{8} \times 58\frac{1}{4}$ *in.* Inscribed: GEORGE. P./TO FRANCIS EARL OF MOIRA. EXH: *R.A.,* 1787 (90). LIT: *A. Graves and W. V. Cronin,* History of the works of Sir J. Reynolds, 4 *vols* (1899–1901), *pp.* 1021–2; *E. K. Waterhouse,* Reynolds (1941), *p.* 79
The Duke of Norfolk

The Prince of Wales is shown in garter robes, attended by a negro servant in hussar uniform. He sat for the portrait in April 1786, and presented it to his friend, the Earl of Moira, later Marquess of Hastings. There is an earlier portrait of him by Reynolds standing by his charger (formerly owned by Lord Brocket), and a half-length portrait in the National Gallery.

George IV. Painting by Sir Thomas Lawrence *(Plate 116)*
Oil on canvas, 114×79 *in.* EXH: *R.A.,* 1822 (74); Kings and Queens, *R. A. Winter,* 1953 (254). LIT: Walpole Society, XXXIX (1962–4), *p.* 87; *O. Millar,* Later Georgian, I, *p.* 61 (873)
Her Majesty the Queen

A reworking of a portrait of George IV when Prince of Wales in garter robes (about 1818, National Gallery of Ireland). The present picture, which is identical in pose and composition, shows the sitter in coronation robes, and was painted towards the end of 1821.

CAROLINE (1768–1821)

Daughter of the Duke of Brunswick. Married George IV when Prince of Wales, 1795, and deserted by him after the birth of Princess Charlotte. Their bitter estrangement culminated in her trial for adultery in the House of Lords, 1820. Ignominiously turned away at the coronation.

Caroline. Bust by Anne Seymour Damer *(Plate 117)*
Terracotta bust, $15\frac{1}{2}$ *in high.* Inscribed: CAROLINE./ PRINCESS./ OF./ WALES./ ANNA. SEYMOUR./ DAMER./ FECIT. 1814. EXH: British Portrait Sculpture during the Neo-Classic Period, *Cyril Humphris,* 1972
Cyril Humphris

Mrs Damer became a professional sculptor after the suicide of her husband, a son of the Earl of Dorchester, in 1776. Well-connected, she executed busts of many prominent personalities.

George IV when Prince of Wales. Painting by Sir Thomas Lawrence *(Plate 118)*
Oil on canvas, $27 \times 20\frac{1}{2}$ *in.* EXH: Lawrence, *R. A. Winter,*

1961 (11). LIT: Walpole Society, XXXIX (1962–4), p. 88
London, National Portrait Gallery

This unfinished sketch is said to have been executed for the coinage, but there is no firm evidence for this. It is related to a drawing in the Royal Collection, datable from a lithograph after it to 1814.

WILLIAM IV (1765–1837) *Reigned* 1830–7

Third son of George III. As Duke of Clarence, pursued a successful career in the navy. Succeeded his brother, George IV. Though not politically astute, he avoided a constitutional crisis by supporting the passage of the first reform bill, 1832.

William IV. Bust by Sir Francis Chantrey *(Plate 119)*
Marble bust, 26 in high. Inscribed : WILLIAM
IV./CHANTREY. FC. 1837. LIT: *Chantrey's 'Ledger' (MS, R.A.), p. 276; Ormond, I, p. 514*
Her Majesty the Queen

Commissioned by William for the Temple of Fame at Kew. It is a version of a popular bust by Chantrey. The original seems to be the marble of 1831 in the collection of Lord de L'Isle and Dudley, and at least another twelve are recorded between that date and 1837 (see Ormond, I, 512–14). Two related drawings, one dated 1830, are in the National Portrait Gallery.

William IV when Duke of Clarence. Study by Sir Thomas Lawrence *(Plate 120)*
Coloured chalks on canvas, 30 × 25 in. LIT: Walpole
Society, XXXIX (1962–4), p. 248, *without present location ;*
O. Millar, Later Georgian, I, p. 62; Ormond, I, p. 512
Sussex, Goodwood House, by courtesy of the Trustees

A study for the full-length portrait in oils by Lawrence of about 1827 in the Royal Collection (Millar, 877). The drawing was engraved by F. C. Lewis and published in 1831.

William IV. Painting by Sir David Wilkie *(Plate 121)*
Oil on canvas, 104 × 68 in. Signed and dated : DAVID
WILKIE F. BRIGHTON. 1833. EXH: *R.A., 1833 (140);*
Wilkie, *R. A. Winter, 1958 (35).* LIT: *A. Cunningham, Life of Sir D. Wilkie (1843), III, p. 50, 54; Ormond, I, p. 513*
London, Apsley House, Wellington Museum

The king is shown in the uniform of the Grenadier Guards. The portrait is said to have been painted from sketches made at Brighton in 1833, although the head is close to that in another full-length by Wilkie of 1832 at Windsor, showing William in garter robes. Wilkie, who was popular with

George IV and his successor, had been appointed principal painter in succession to Lawrence, 1830.

ADELAIDE (1792–1849)

Eldest daughter of the Duke of Saxe-Coburg-Meiningen. Married William, Duke of Clarence, later William IV, 1818, and became queen on his accession, 1830.

Adelaide. Painting by Sir Martin Archer Shee *(Plate 122)*
Oil on canvas, 99½ × 63¾ in. EXH: *R.A., 1837 (68).* LIT:
O. Millar, Later Georgian, I, p. 116 (1085)
Her Majesty the Queen

Originally commissioned by the Goldsmiths Company, but retained by William IV. Shee, the president of the Royal Academy, had painted the king in 1833.

VICTORIA (1819–1901) *Reigned* 1837–1901

Daughter of the Duke of Kent, and granddaughter of George III. Succeeded her uncle, William IV. Married Prince Albert of Saxe-Coburg Gotha, 1840. Influenced to a considerable extent the foreign and home policies of successive governments, and the manners and attitudes of her people. Her reign, the longest in British history, saw the consolidation of the Empire, the expansion of industry and commerce, and numerous reforms in the spheres of government, and social welfare.

ALBERT (1819–61)

Second son of the Duke of Saxe-Coburg Gotha. Married his cousin, Victoria, 1840, and created Prince Consort. Played an influential role in public affairs. A noted collector and patron of the arts. Largely responsible for the Great Exhibition of 1851.

The Coronation of Victoria. Detail of engraving by H. T. Ryall after Sir George Hayter *(Plate 123)*
Engraving, 22½ × 34¼ in. LIT: *Ormond, I, p. 481*
London, National Portrait Gallery

An engraving after Hayter's well-known picture in the Royal Collection, showing the climax of the coronation ceremony (28 June 1838). The queen has just been crowned, and the onlookers are acclaiming her with shouts of 'God save the Queen'. Prominent among them are Wellington and Melbourne.

Windsor Castle in modern times. Painting by Sir Edwin Landseer *(Plate 124)*

Oil on canvas, 44½ × 56½ in. EXH: Landseer, *R. A. Winter,* 1961 (95); Landseer and his World, *Mappin Art Gallery, Sheffield,* 1972 (79); British Sporting Painting, *Arts Council,* 1974 (187). LIT: *A. Graves,* Catalogue of the Works of . . . Sir Edwin Landseer (1876), *p.* 25 (318); *Ormond,* 1, *p.* 484

Her Majesty the Queen

The picture is set in 1842, and shows Prince Albert on his return from hunting, with Victoria and the Princess Royal; the dogs are the greyhound, Eos, and the skye terriers, Dandie, Islay and Carnach. In the garden the Duchess of Kent and a companion can be seen wheeling the Prince of Wales in a pram. Although the picture is domestic in character, it is carefully stage-managed. Prince Albert, in immaculate clothes, looks like the hero in a contemporary opera (Weber's *Der Freischütz* has been suggested), and the dead game includes ptarmigan, which can only be shot north of the border. Queen Victoria records in her diary (Royal Archives) for 2 October 1845: 'Landseer's Game Picture (begun in 1840!) with us 2, Vicky . . . is at last hung up in our sitting room here, and is a very beautiful picture, and altogether very cheerful and pleasing.' A related oil study of Victoria and Albert of 1839 is at Windsor.

Victoria and Albert. Painting by F. X. Winterhalter *(Plate 125)*

Oil on canvas, 22½ × 17½ in. Signed and dated : FX WINTERHALTER 1851. EXH: British Portraits, *R. A. Winter,* 1956–7 (715)

Her Majesty the Queen

Dressed as Catherine of Braganza and Charles II for a *bal costumé* held at Buckingham Palace on 13 June 1851. The queen records the price of the picture, a hundred guineas, in her account book (Royal Archives, T.232, p. 5).

Victoria and Albert dressed as Anglo-Saxons. Statue by William Theed *(Plate 126)*

Plaster statue, 78 in high. LIT: *Ormond,* 1, *p.* 489

Her Majesty the Queen, on loan to the National Portrait Gallery

This is the model for the marble statue at Windsor of 1868. It exemplifies the posthumous cult of Prince Albert so carefully nurtured by the queen (he is pointing the way to heaven, where she will soon follow him). The heroic simplicity of the Anglo-Saxons appealed deeply to the Victorian imagination, and it finds expression in their literature and art from the 1840s onwards.

Victoria and Albert. Painting by Sir Edwin Landseer *(Plate 127)*

Oil on canvas, 55¼ × 42¾ in. EXH: Landseer, *R. A. Winter,* 1961 (94); La Peinture Romantique Anglaise, *Petit Palais, Paris,* 1972 (156). LIT: *A. Graves, op. cit., p.* 25; *Ormond,* 1, *p.* 484

Her Majesty the Queen

The royal couple are dressed as Queen Philippa and Edward III for a *bal costumé* held at Buckingham Palace, 12 May 1842. It is illustrated and described at length in the first number of the *Illustrated London News* (14 May 1842).

Victoria. Painting by F. X. Winterhalter *(Plate 128)*

Oil on canvas, 25⅝ × 20⅞ in (oval). Signed : F. WINTERHALTER. LIT: *Ormond,* 1, *p.* 485

Her Majesty the Queen

A romantic portrait of the queen with unbraided hair, commissioned by her in 1843 as a birthday present for Prince Albert. She sat for what she called the 'secret' or 'surprise' picture on 8, 10 and 13 July, writing in her diary (Royal Archives) that it is 'to my joy succeeding very well'. It was given to Albert on 26 August and remained his favourite portrait of her. The price of a hundred guineas is recorded in the queen's account book (Royal Archives, T.231, *p.* 58).

Victoria with the Princess Royal. Calotype attributed to Henry Collen *(Plate 129)*

Her Majesty the Queen

The earliest recorded photograph of the queen, dating from about 1844–5.

'The First of May, 1851.' Painting by F. X. Winterhalter *(Plate 130)*

Oil on canvas, 42 × 51 in. Signed and dated : F WINTERHALTER 1851. EXH: King's Pictures, *R. A. Winter,* 1946–7 (56); Paintings and Drawings by Victorian Artists, *National Gallery of Canada, Ottawa,* 1965 (171); Victorian Paintings, *Mappin Art Gallery, Sheffield,* 1968 (151). LIT: *C. H. Collins Baker,* Catalogue of the Principal Pictures at Windsor Castle (1937), *p.* 316; *Ormond,* 1, *p.* 487

Her Majesty the Queen

Painted to celebrate the first birthday of Prince Arthur, later Duke of Connaught (born 1 May 1850). Held by his mother, he is being presented with a casket by his godfather, the Duke of Wellington, while Prince Albert is shown behind on the right. The imagery of the figure composition suggests an adoration scene, while in the background the Crystal Palace stands for modern progress. Queen Victoria records in her diary (Royal Archives) for 21 May 1851 that 'dear Albert with his wonderful knowledge and taste' had given the artist 'the idea which is now to be carried out'. In a second reference (29 May), she writes that Winterhalter is 'quite engrossed' in his first of May picture.

Victoria and her family. Calotype by Roger Fenton *(Plate 131)*
Her Majesty the Queen

One of a remarkable group of family photographs taken by Fenton in 1854. The queen has her arm around Princess Alice, while standing on the left are the Prince of Wales and the Princess Royal, and Prince Alfred on the right.

Victoria with the Prince and Princess of Wales. Photograph by J. P. Mayall *(Plate 132)*
London, National Portrait Gallery

One of an extraordinary series of photographs showing the queen in mourning for Prince Albert, dating from 1863.

Edward VII when Prince of Wales with his wife and children. Painting by Heinrich von Angeli *(Plate 133)*
Oil on canvas, 65 × 53¼ in. Signed: H. V. ANGELI
Her Majesty the Queen

A family group of about 1876 showing Edward with his eldest son, Albert, Duke of Clarence, and Alexandra holding Princess Maud. They are grouped by a colonnade with a view of Sandringham, the prince's country house, in the background. Von Angeli entered royal service on the recommendation of the Princess Royal, and he became Queen Victoria's favourite painter. It is significant that, like Winterhalter, her earlier favourite, he was German.

A Vision. Woodcut by an Unknown Artist *(Plate 134)*
From The Razor; or London Humorist and Satirist, 11 *July* 1868

The ghost of Elizabeth I confronts the Widow of Windsor, and bids her do her duty. Victoria's long seclusion from public life, following Albert's death, was the subject of fierce criticism. The juxtaposition of images in the print is interesting.

Victoria with an Indian attendant at Frogmore. Photograph by Hills & Saunders *(Plate 135)*
London, National Portrait Gallery

A delightful and telling image of the ageing Queen Victoria, signing state papers under an awning at Frogmore. With her is one of her Indian servants, to whom she was devoted.

The royal family at the time of the Jubilee. Painting by Laurits Tuxen *(Plate 136)*
Oil on canvas, 63 × 87 in. Signed and dated: L TUXEN 1887. EXH: *St James's Gallery, King St., May* 1888; *Victorian Exhibition, New Gallery,* 1891–2 (70). LIT: *Ormond,* I, p. 490
Her Majesty the Queen

Painted at the time of the queen's Jubilee in 1887. Tuxen, a Danish artist, had already worked for the Danish royal family, and no doubt he owed his introduction to Victoria to them. He later painted the wedding of the Duke of York, later George V, and Princess Mary, and a view of the Diamond Jubilee procession. The 1887 group cost a thousand pounds. A photogravure after it was published by Mendoza, proprietor of the St James's Gallery.

The four generations. Photograph by W. & D. Downey *(Plate 137)*
Her Majesty the Queen

Queen Victoria is holding Prince Edward, later Edward VIII, at his christening, White Lodge, Richmond Park, 1894. On the left is the Prince of Wales, later Edward VII, and on the right the Duke of York, later George V.

EDWARD VII (1841–1910) *Reigned* 1901–10

Eldest son of Victoria, whom he succeeded. Married Princess Alexandra, 1863. Reacted against his severely moral and intellectual upbringing, becoming a leader of fashionable society and something of a libertine. Distrusted by his mother, who prevented him from playing any effective role in public affairs. During his brief reign proved to be an exemplary and popular monarch.

Edward VII. Painting by Sir Arthur S. Cope *(Plates 138 and 139)*
Oil on canvas, 50 × 36 in. Obscurely signed and dated 1907. EXH: *R.A.,* 1907 (161): Kings and Queens, *R. A. Winter,* 1953 (278)
The Earl Mountbatten of Burma

The most successful state portrait of the king, showing him in garter robes. It was given by the sitter to his friend, Sir Ernest Cassel, and several copies were made for embassies.

The three generations. Press photograph *(Plate 140)*

Edward VII, with his son, the future George V, and his grandson, the future Edward VIII, taken on board the royal yacht in 1909. This was one of the last photographs of the king.

Edward VII on his deathbed. Sketch by John Singer Sargent *(Plate 141)*
Black chalk on paper, 17⅝ × 23⅛ in. Signed and dated: JOHN S. SARGENT MAY 8TH 1910
Her Majesty the Queen

Sargent had declined the commission to paint Edward VII's coronation (given to his friend, Edwin Abbey), and this is his only portrait of the king. The latter had died shortly before midnight on 6 May 1910.

GEORGE V (1865–1936) *Reigned 1910–36*

Second son of Edward VII. His naval career cut short by the death of his elder brother, 1892. Married Princess Mary of Teck, 1893. Despite his political inexperience, overcame several constitutional crises at the start of his reign. Won the hearts of his people by his unaffected simplicity and devotion to duty.

QUEEN MARY (1867–1953)

Daughter of the Duke of Teck. Engaged to the Duke of Clarence, and, after his death, married his brother, the Duke of York, later George V. Became queen consort, 1910. A woman of great character, she devoted her life to the service of the monarchy. Noted as a connoisseur and collector.

Queen Mary and Queen Alexandra. Photograph by Mrs Albert Broom *(Plate 142)*
London, National Portrait Gallery

Taken in 1915, the occasion is not recorded. Alexandra was the widowed wife of Edward VII.

The Delhi Durbar. Press photograph *(Plate 143)*

The Delhi Durbar of 1911 was the only ceremonial occasion in India attended by the reigning monarch. The Indian princes paid homage to their recently crowned king-emperor, George V, accompanied by Queen Mary.

The royal family at Buckingham Palace. Painting by Sir John Lavery *(Plate 144)*
Oil on canvas, 134 × 107 in. Signed and dated :
J LAVERY/13. EXH: *R.A.*, 1913 (170). LIT : *J. Lavery*, The Life of a Painter (1940), *p. 159*
London, National Portrait Gallery, by courtesy of R. A. Spottiswoode

George V and Queen Mary are shown in the White Drawing Room at Buckingham Palace, with their two eldest children, the Prince of Wales, later Edward VIII, and the Princess Royal, later Countess of Harewood. The queen asked Lavery to provide a sketch of the intended grouping, and it was her idea that the picture should include only two of her children. Lavery made studies at Buckingham Palace, but the large picture was finished in his studio. The picture was commissioned by W. H. Spottiswoode for presentation to the nation, with the approval of the king and queen.

George V. Painting by Sir Arthur S. Cope *(Plate 145)*
Oil on canvas, 95 × 59½ in. Signed and dated : A S COPE 1913. EXH : *R.A.*, 1913 (192)
London, United Service and Royal Aero Club

The king is shown on the deck of a battleship, with a view of the Grand Fleet behind, in the uniform of an admiral. The portrait was commissioned by the club, together with a companion portrait of Queen Mary by Sir William Llewellyn. Cope painted several later portraits of the king for, among others, the Royal College of Music (1926), the Royal Collection (1927), and the Royal Academy (1928).

George V. Press photograph *(Plate 146)*
Taken at the Cenotaph during Remembrance Sunday, 1920.

A conversation piece at Aintree. Painting by W. R. Sickert *(Plate 147)*
Oil on canvas, 18½ × 18¼ in. Inscribed, signed and dated : BY COURTESY OF TOPICAL P[RESS]/AGENCY 11 + 12 RED LION/COURT E.C.4./AINTREE. 25.3.27./SICKERT.
EXH : *London Group*, 1931 ; *Beaux Arts Gallery*, 1932 (31).
LIT : *W. Baron*, Sickert (1973), *pp. 381–2 (under 408)*
Her Majesty Queen Elizabeth the Queen Mother

Based on the photograph reproduced as Plate 148. Wendy Baron puts the painting towards the end of the date bracket, 1927–30. In 1931, the portrait was rejected by the authorities of the Glasgow Art Gallery as insufficiently majestic. Sickert painted another portrait of George V with Queen Mary, on a Jubilee drive in 1935, again based on a press photograph.

George V with his trainer, Major Featherstonhaugh, at Aintree. Press photograph *(Plate 148)*
Taken on 24 March 1927, and used by Sickert as the basis for his painting *(Plate 147)*.

George V. Press photograph *(Plate 149)*
A rare view of the king smiling. The date and occasion are not recorded.

EDWARD VIII (1894–1972) *Reigned 1936*

A popular Prince of Wales, noted for his informality of approach, and his keen concern with current social problems. Succeeded his father, George V, but forced to abdicate when he refused to give up the twice divorced Mrs Simpson. Thenceforth lived mostly in retirement abroad. (*See notes to Plates 154 and 155 opposite.*)

GEORGE VI (1895–1952) *Reigned 1936–52*

Created Duke of York, 1920. Succeeded to the throne on the abdication of his brother, Edward VIII. Retiring and diffident by temperament, he accepted the responsibilities of his office, and played a full role in the affairs of the country during years of war and crisis. Much loved and respected.

QUEEN ELIZABETH THE QUEEN MOTHER (*born* 1900)

Youngest daughter of the 14th Earl of Strathmore. Married the Duke of York, later George VI, 1923. Became queen consort, 1936, and Queen Mother on the death of her husband, 1952. A radiant personality, and enormously popular.

Queen Elizabeth the Queen Mother when Lady Elizabeth Bowes-Lyon. Photograph by Vandyk (*Plate 150*)

Taken shortly before the announcement of her engagement to the Duke of York, later George VI, in 1922.

Queen Elizabeth the Queen Mother when Duchess of York. Painting by Philip de Laszlo (*Plate 151*)
Oil on canvas, 37 × 29 in. Signed and dated 1925
Her Majesty the Queen

One of several portraits of the Queen Mother. The first was painted in 1925 for her mother, Lady Strathmore.

The Royal Family, 1923. Photograph by Bassano (*Plate 152*)
London, National Portrait Gallery

George V and Queen Mary with Princess Mary, the Princess Royal, and their four sons, the Prince of Wales, later Edward VIII, the Duke of Gloucester, the Duke of York, later George VI, and the Duke of Kent. A typical studio group photograph of its period.

George VI and Queen Elizabeth the Queen Mother when Duke and Duchess of York. Press photograph (*Plate 153*)

Taken at Bethnal Green, November 1929.

Edward VIII when Prince of Wales at miners' cottages in Northumberland. Press photograph (*Plate 154*)

Taken in 1929.

Edward VIII. Painting by W. R. Sickert (*Plate 155*)
Oil on canvas, 72 × 36 in. Signed: SICKERT. EXH: Leicester Galleries, 1936 (129). LIT: W. Baron, Sickert (1973), p. 382 (409)
Fredericton, New Brunswick. Beaverbrook Canadian Foundation, Beaverbrook Art Gallery

Based on a photograph by Harold Clements, showing Edward VIII in the uniform of the Welsh Guards arriving at a church parade service of the regiment on St David's Day, 1 March 1936. The painting attracted considerable publicity as the first exhibited portrait of the new king, and it was praised as a likeness.

George VI. Painting by Sir Gerald Kelly (*Plate 156*)
Oil on canvas, 107 × 68 in. EXH: R.A., 1945 (159). LIT: D. Hudson, For Love of Painting: the Life of Sir Gerald Kelly (1975), pp. 60–72
Her Majesty the Queen

Commissioned in 1938, with a companion picture of Queen Elizabeth the Queen Mother, as the first official state portraits. Both sitters are in coronation robes. A study of the head and hands of the king's picture was painted at Windsor in April 1939, and Kelly originally hoped to finish the portraits by the end of that year. In the event, he spent a further six years at work on them, occupying a special studio at Windsor throughout the war. The history of the state portraits is described at length by Hudson. He says that Kelly regarded them as the most important commission of his career, and that 'An absolute determination to make them a success alerted his complex apparatus of craftsmanship and, with it, his meticulous, almost pedantic, sense of accuracy'. The original sketch for the king's picture was presented by the artist to the British Institute, Florence, and a great many related variants and copies are known.

Queen Elizabeth the Queen Mother. Photograph by Cecil Beaton (*Plate 157*)
By courtesy of Cecil Beaton

From a group of photographs taken in 1940. The painted background is based on Fragonard's picture of *The Swing*.

George VI and Queen Elizabeth the Queen Mother with Her Majesty the Queen when Princess Elizabeth, and Princess Margaret. Press photograph (*Plate 158*)

Taken at Bertram Mills Circus, December 1934.

Queen Mary with Her Majesty the Queen when Princess Elizabeth. Press photograph (*Plate 159*)

Taken outside the entrance to the National Portrait Gallery, March 1938.

Harvest at Sandringham. Press photograph (*Plate 160*)

Taken in August 1943. The royal family are inspecting Sandringham Park, which had been ploughed up under the wartime food production policy.

Queen Elizabeth the Queen Mother inspecting the Citizens' Advice Bureau. Press photograph (*Plate 161*)

Taken in July 1942.

George VI with Her Majesty the Queen when Princess Elizabeth. Press photograph *(Plate 162)*

Taken at the Cenotaph, Remembrance Sunday, 1945. The princess is in the uniform of an Auxiliary Territorial Service junior commander.

HER MAJESTY QUEEN ELIZABETH II *(born 1926)*.
Queen regnant since 1952

Elder daughter of George VI. Married Prince Philip, 20 November 1947. Succeeded to the throne on the death of her father. With the help of her husband, she has kept the monarchy in tune with the spirit of the times, without sacrificing its essential traditions. Though burdened with official duties, she has brought up a family of four children, and kept alive her interest in country pursuits.

PRINCE PHILIP, DUKE OF EDINBURGH *(born 1921)*

Only son of Prince Andrew of Greece. Educated in Great Britain, and naturalized as a British subject. Pursued a successful naval career, like his grandfather, Prince Louis Mountbatten. He married Princess Elizabeth, now Elizabeth II, 20 November 1947, and was created Duke of Edinburgh. A forceful and outgoing personality, he has been associated with numerous causes and projects, cultural, sporting and environmental. He has made his views known on current topics, and he has helped to bring the monarchy into touch with the contemporary world.

PRINCESS MARGARET, COUNTESS OF SNOWDON *(born 1930)*

Younger daughter of George VI. Though inevitably overshadowed by her elder sister, she has impressed her style, good looks and individuality on the public. In 1960, she married Anthony Armstrong-Jones, later Earl of Snowdon, from whom she is now separated. They have two children.

Princess Margaret at a fashion show. Press photograph *(Plate 163)*
By courtesy of the Press Association

Taken in March 1951. The princess's coat was designed by Norman Hartnell.

Her Majesty the Queen when Princess Elizabeth, and Prince Philip. Press photograph *(Plate 164)*

Taken shortly before their wedding, 1947.

The christening of Prince Michael of Kent. Press photograph *(Plate 165)*

Taken in 1942. See the caption for a key.

Silver Wedding group. Photograph by Patrick Lichfield *(Plate 166)*
By courtesy of Patrick Lichfield

A picture of the entire royal family taken to commemorate the silver wedding of Her Majesty the Queen and Prince Philip on 20 November 1972. See the caption for a key.

Her Majesty Queen Elizabeth II. Painting by Pietro Annigoni *(Plates 1 and 167)*
Oil on canvas, 59 × 39¼ in. Inscribed : IN LONDRA. A.M.G.P./LIV/LV. EXH : *R.A., 1955 (227); British Portraits, R. A. Winter, 1956–7 (799).* LIT : *N. Rasmo, Pietro Annigoni (Florence, 1961), Plate 83*
London, Fishmongers' Company

Commissioned in 1954 and finished the following year. The Queen is dressed in garter robes and posed against a winter landscape. A study is reproduced in Rasmo, reverse of title page. A companion portrait of Prince Philip was painted in 1956, and a later portrait of Her Majesty the Queen by Annigoni of 1970 is in the National Portrait Gallery.

Her Majesty Queen Elizabeth II. Photograph by Cecil Beaton *(Plate 168)*
By courtesy of Cecil Beaton

Taken in the throne room at Buckingham Palace soon after the coronation, 2 June 1953. The Queen wears coronation robes and the imperial crown, and carries the orb and sceptre.

Her Majesty Queen Elizabeth II. Press photograph *(Plate 169)*

Her Majesty the Queen on her way to the House of Lords for the state opening of parliament, 1953.

Her Majesty Queen Elizabeth II talking to Mrs Winifred Gaskin. Press photograph *(Plate 170)*

Taken during the royal tour of the Caribbean, February 1966. Mrs Gaskin was British Guiana's Education Minister.

Her Majesty the Queen when Princess Elizabeth. Press photograph *(Plate 171)*

Taken on board the royal train in Alberta, Canada, 1949.

Her Majesty Queen Elizabeth II with Prince Andrew and Prince Edward. Photograph by Cecil Beaton *(Plate 172)*
By courtesy of Cecil Beaton

Taken in 1964, the year of Prince Edward's birth. Prince Andrew was born in 1960.

PRINCE CHARLES, PRINCE OF WALES (*born* 1948)

Eldest son of Her Majesty the Queen and Prince Philip. An extrovert like his father, he has established himself in the public eye as a delightful and expansive personality. He has a very wide range of interests, and is outstanding among members of the royal family for his considerable sympathy with the arts.

Prince Charles and Prince Edward. Still from a television film *(Plate 173)*
By courtesy of the Incorporated Television Company

From the 1969 film on the royal family.

PRINCESS ANNE (*born* 1950)

Only daughter of Her Majesty the Queen and Prince Philip. A strong-minded personality, she has caught the imagination of the public with her feats as a horsewoman. She married Captain Mark Phillips in 1973.

Princess Anne. Press photograph *(Plate 174)*
Taken at Swan Hunter's Shipyard, during the launching of the tanker, *Esso Northumbria*, May 1969.

Princess Anne. Detail of painting by Michael Noakes *(Plate 175)*
Oil on canvas, 25 × 30 *in. Signed and dated :* MICHAEL NOAKES 1973. EXH: *R.A.,* 1973 (8)
Private collection

One of the most successful recent studies of Princess Anne by the well-known portrait painter and art critic.

Princess Anne. Photograph by Norman Parkinson *(Plate 176)*
By courtesy of Norman Parkinson

One of a group of photographs taken in 1971.

The Investiture of the Prince of Wales. Press photograph *(Plate 177)*
Prince Charles, heir to the throne, being formally invested with the insignia of the Prince of Wales at Caernarvon Castle on 1 July 1969. The castle was built by Edward I, father of the first Prince of Wales.

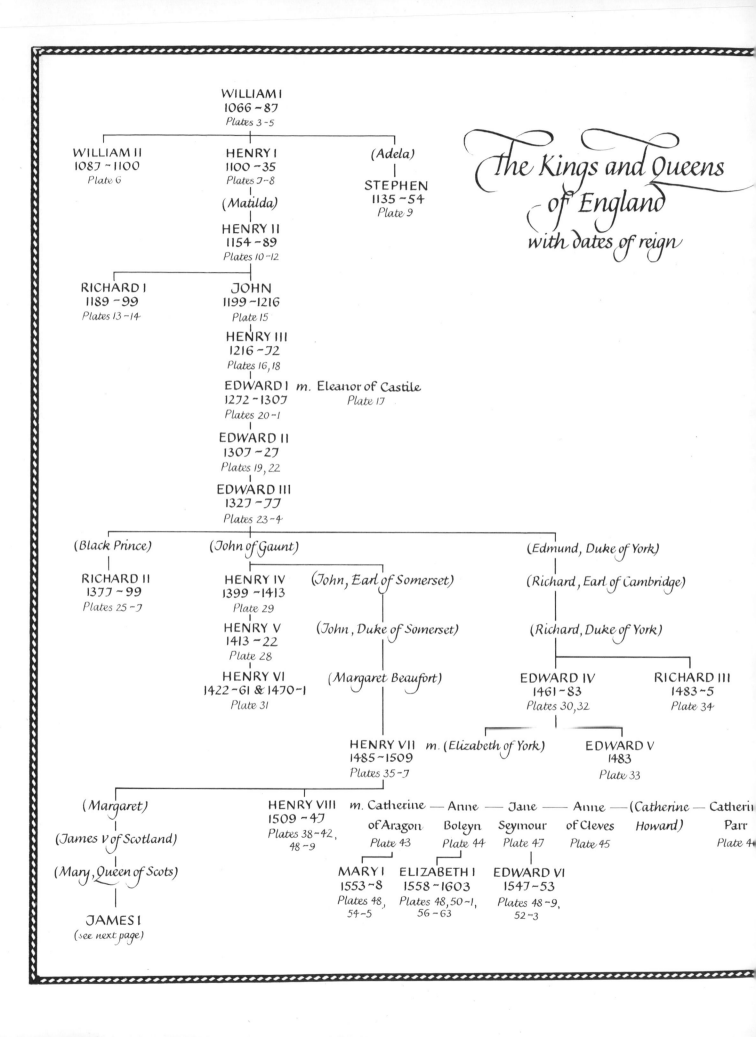

WILLIAM I
1066 ~ 87
Plates 3 - 5

WILLIAM II
1087 ~ 1100
Plate 6

HENRY I
1100 ~ 35
Plates 7 - 8

(Adela)

STEPHEN
1135 ~ 54
Plate 9

(Matilda)

HENRY II
1154 ~ 89
Plates 10 - 12

The Kings and Queens of England
with dates of reign

RICHARD I
1189 ~ 99
Plates 13 - 14

JOHN
1199 ~ 1216
Plate 15

HENRY III
1216 ~ 72
Plates 16, 18

EDWARD I *m.* Eleanor of Castile
1272 ~ 1307   *Plate 17*
Plates 20 - 1

EDWARD II
1307 ~ 27
Plates 19, 22

EDWARD III
1327 ~ 77
Plates 23 - 4

(Black Prince)

(John of Gaunt)

(Edmund, Duke of York)

RICHARD II
1377 ~ 99
Plates 25 - 7

HENRY IV
1399 ~ 1413
Plate 29

(John, Earl of Somerset)

(Richard, Earl of Cambridge)

HENRY V
1413 ~ 22
Plate 28

(John, Duke of Somerset)

(Richard, Duke of York)

HENRY VI
1422 ~ 61 & 1470 ~ 1
Plate 31

(Margaret Beaufort)

EDWARD IV
1461 ~ 83
Plates 30, 32

RICHARD III
1483 ~ 5
Plate 34

HENRY VII *m.* (Elizabeth of York)
1485 ~ 1509
Plates 35 - 7

EDWARD V
1483
Plate 33

(Margaret)

HENRY VIII
1509 ~ 47
Plates 38 - 42,
48 - 9

m. Catherine —— Anne —— Jane —— Anne —— (Catherine — Catherine
of Aragon   Boleyn   Seymour   of Cleves   Howard)   Parr

Plate 43   *Plate 44*   *Plate 47*   *Plate 45*   *Plate 46*

(James V of Scotland)

(Mary, Queen of Scots)

MARY I
1553 ~ 8
Plates 48,
54 - 5

ELIZABETH I
1558 ~ 1603
Plates 48, 50 - 1,
56 - 63

EDWARD VI
1547 ~ 53
Plates 48 - 9,
52 - 3

JAMES I
(see next page)

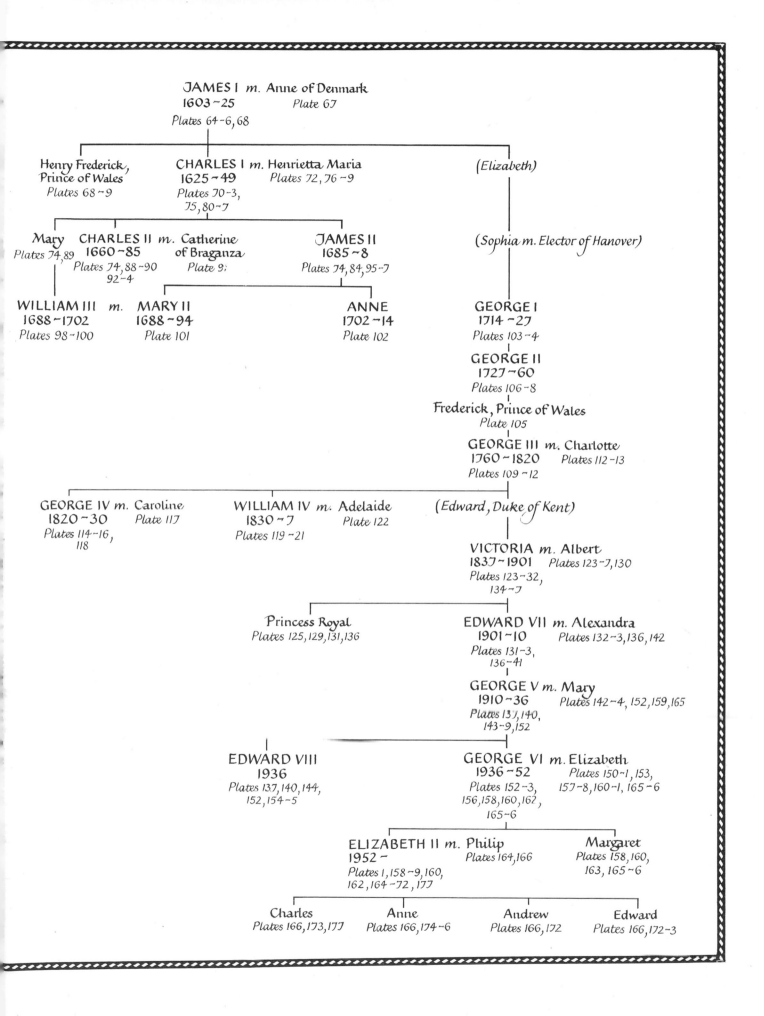

JAMES I *m.* Anne of Denmark
1603~25   *Plate 67*
Plates 64~6, 68

Henry Frederick,   CHARLES I *m.* Henrietta Maria   (*Elizabeth*)
Prince of Wales   1625~49   *Plates 72, 76~9*
Plates 68~9   *Plates 70~3,*
                        75, 80~7

Mary   CHARLES II *m.* Catherine   JAMES II   (*Sophia m. Elector of Hanover*)
Plates 74, 89   1660~85   of Braganza   1685~8
              Plates 74, 88~90   *Plate 9.*   *Plates 74, 84, 95~7*
                 92~4

WILLIAM III   *m.*   MARY II   ANNE   GEORGE I
1688~1702   1688~94   1702~14   1714~27
Plates 98~100   *Plate 101*   *Plate 102*   *Plates 103~4*

                                        GEORGE II
                                        1727~60
                                        Plates 106~8

                                Frederick, Prince of Wales
                                        Plate 105

                                GEORGE III *m.* Charlotte
                                1760~1820   *Plates 112~13*
                                Plates 109~12

GEORGE IV *m.* Caroline   WILLIAM IV *m.* Adelaide   (*Edward, Duke of Kent*)
1820~30   *Plate 117*   1830~7   *Plate 122*
Plates 114~16,   *Plates 119~21*
118

                                        VICTORIA *m.* Albert
                                        1837~1901   *Plates 123~7, 130*
                                        Plates 123~32,
                                        134~7

              Princess Royal   EDWARD VII *m.* Alexandra
              Plates 125, 129, 131, 136   1901~10   *Plates 132~3, 136, 142*
                                        Plates 131~3,
                                        136~41

                                        GEORGE V *m.* Mary
                                        1910~36   *Plates 142~4, 152, 159, 165*
                                        Plates 137, 140,
                                        143~9, 152

              EDWARD VIII   GEORGE VI *m.* Elizabeth
              1936   1936~52   *Plates 150~1, 153,*
              Plates 137, 140, 144,   *Plates 152~3,*   *157~8, 160~1, 165~6*
              152, 154~5   *156, 158, 160, 162,*
                                  165~6

                   ELIZABETH II *m.* Philip   Margaret
                   1952~   *Plates 164, 166*   *Plates 158, 160,*
                   Plates 1, 158~9, 160,   *163, 165~6*
                   162, 164~72, 177

Charles   Anne   Andrew   Edward
Plates 166, 173, 177   *Plates 166, 174~6*   *Plates 166, 172*   *Plates 166, 172~3*

Acknowledgements

PLATES 31, 32, 34, 38, 41, 51, 53, 65, 66, 71, 72, 74, 75, 76, 77, 78, 79, 82, 83, 89, 90, 91, 108, 109, 112, 113, 116, 119, 122, 124, 125, 126, 127, 128, 129, 130, 131, 133, 136, 137, 141, 151, 156 are reproduced by gracious permission of Her Majesty the Queen.

The publishers are grateful to the following for kindly providing photographs. The names of the owners by courtesy of whom these photographs are reproduced are given in the notes to the plates.

Cecil Beaton : 157, 168, 172
Beaverbrook Canadian Foundation, Fredericton : 155
Bildarchiv Foto Marburg : 11, 14, 22
British Library : 4, 7, 20, 29, 30
British Museum : 5, 6, 8, 9, 10, 21, 50, 70
Camera Press : 166, 176
Caisse Nationale des Monuments Historiques et des sites, Paris : 12, 13
Christ Church, Oxford : 104
Clichés des Musées Nationaux, Paris : 45
Cooper-Bridgeman Library : 28, 84
Courtauld Institute : 57, 64, 111
Charles Howard, Chichester : 120
Cyril Humphris : 117
Incorporated Television Company Ltd : 173
A. F. Kersting : 15, 19
Kunsthistorisches Museum, Vienna : 47
Metropolitan Museum of Art, New York : 69
National Gallery, London : 25, 26 (courtesy the Dean and Chapter of Westminster), 39
National Gallery of Art, Washington : 52

National Maritime Museum, Greenwich : 95, 96
National Monuments Record : 16 (Crown copyright), 17 and 18 (copyright Warburg Institute), 103 (copyright Warburg Institute, photo Helmut Gernsheim)
National Portrait Gallery : 23 (courtesy Dean and Chapter of Westminster), 35, 42, 43, 44, 46, 48, 49, 58, 59, 60, 67, 68, 73, 81 (courtesy Victoria and Albert Museum), 85, 86, 87, 88, 93, 94, 97, 99 (courtesy Rijksmuseum, Amsterdam), 100 (courtesy Victoria and Albert Museum), 105, 107, 114, 118, 123, 132, 134, 135, 142, 144, 145, 152, 171 (from H. Tatlock Miller and Loudon Sainthill : *Undoubted Queen*)
National Portrait Gallery (Daily Herald Library) : 140, 146, 148, 149, 150, 153, 154, 158, 159, 160, 161, 162, 164, 170, 174
National Portrait Gallery (Planet News) : 169
National Trust : 98
Terence Pepper : 143
Phaidon Press Archives : 1, 3, 27, 33 (courtesy Dean and Chapter of Canterbury), 37 (copyright Warburg Institute), 56, 63, 106, 115, 138, 139, 147, 167
Popperphoto : 165
Prado, Madrid : 54, 55
Press Association : 163, 177
Royal Academy : 51, 80, 175 (courtesy Michael Noakes)
Scottish National Portrait Gallery : 110
Victoria and Albert Museum : 36, 61, 62, 92, 101 (courtesy Dean and Chapter of Westminster), 121
Walker Art Gallery, Liverpool : 40
Weidenfeld & Nicolson (photograph by Werner Forman) : 2
Dean and Chapter of Westminster : 24
Jeremy Whitaker : 102

Index